Voice of Barak Valley
(Assam)

AF517276

Unheard Stories,
Unspoken Truths from
The Soul of Southern Assam

Muazzaz Ahmed Choudhury (Faaiz)

First Edition: 2025
Paperback Published by Pothi in India and Globally via Amazon Kindle Direct Publishing (KDP), Lulu & Draft2Digital.

ISBN (Paperback): 978-93-343-4499-8
ISBN (eBook): 978-93-343-5468-3
Cover Design & Layout: Muazzaz Ahmed Choudhury

Distribution & Availability Rights

Voice of Barak Valley is published under the full and independent distribution rights of the author.

The paperback edition, carrying the author's official ISBN, is available in India via Amazon.in, Flipkart, Pothi Store, and internationally through Lulu Bookstore & major Amazon marketplaces including the US, UK, NL, Germany, France, Italy, Spain, Japan, Canada, Australia, Poland, Sweden, Brazil, and Mexico.

The eBook edition is published under the author's ownership & is available globally on platforms such as Amazon Kindle Store, Google Play Books, Apple Books & other supported e-reading platforms.

Both editions are catalogued using the author's own ISBNs and are eligible for acquisition by:

•Libraries and educational institutions
•Academic retailers and bookstores
•Digital and print distribution networks

For rights, licensing, or distribution inquiries, please contact: faaiz.choudhuryy@gmail.com

Disclaimer

This book is a work of nonfiction based on factual records, personal recollections, oral history, and cultural narratives from the Barak Valley region of Assam, India. While every effort has been made to ensure accuracy, certain names, dates, and accounts may reflect personal interpretations or traditional storytelling. The author does not claim to represent every possible version of historical events or community perspectives. This book is intended for educational and cultural reflection purposes. Any resemblance to individuals, communities, or events not explicitly documented is purely coincidental or interpretative.

The author holds no liability for the use or interpretation of the content within this publication.

– Muazzaz Ahmed Choudhury
Author, Voice of Barak Valley

অস্বীকৃতি

এই গ্রন্থটি একটি প্রামাণ্য অ-সাহিত্যিক রচনা, যা আসামের বরাক উপত্যকার ইতিহাস, ঐতিহ্য, মৌখিক স্মৃতি এবং পারিবারিক ও সাংস্কৃতিক বর্ণনার উপর ভিত্তি করে রচিত। এতে ব্যবহৃত সমস্ত তথ্য, স্থান ও ঘটনা যথাসম্ভব গবেষণালব্ধ ও নির্ভরযোগ্য উৎস থেকে সংগৃহীত হয়েছে। তথ্য উপস্থাপনের ক্ষেত্রে যথাযথ সতর্কতা অবলম্বন করা হয়েছে, তবে কিছু নাম, তারিখ ও ঘটনা লেখকের ব্যক্তিগত অভিজ্ঞতা, স্মৃতি বা ঐতিহ্যবাহী কথনের জনশ্রুতির মাধ্যমে উপস্থাপিত হতে পারে। এই গ্রন্থে উপস্থাপিত প্রতিটি ঘটনার ব্যাখ্যা সর্বজনগ্রাহ্য বা চূড়ান্ত ইতিহাস হিসেবে গণ্য করার অনুরোধ করা হচ্ছে না। গ্রন্থটি মূলত শিক্ষা, গবেষণা ও সাংস্কৃতিক চিন্তাচর্চার উদ্দেশ্যে রচিত। এখানে বর্ণিত কোনো ব্যক্তি, সম্প্রদায় বা ঘটনার সঙ্গে বাস্তবের সাদৃশ্য সম্পূর্ণ কাকতালীয় বা ব্যাখ্যামূলক হতে পারে।

এই প্রকাশনায় অন্তর্ভুক্ত তথ্যের ব্যবহার বা ব্যাখ্যার জন্য লেখক কোনো প্রকার আইনগত দায়ভার গ্রহণ করবেন না।

– মুয়াজ্জাজ আহমদ চৌধুরী
লেখক, ভয়েস অফ বরাক ভ্যালি

Preface

History is not always written in ink, it often survives in memory, in spoken words passed down through generations, in fading documents, and in the quiet pride of communities that remember what others have chosen to forget. This book is born from such memory and silence. It is an attempt to record, preserve, and honour the complex socio-political journey of the Barak Valley and its people, especially those who stood at the frontlines of change, resistance, and identity.

What began as a personal inquiry soon grew into a much larger pursuit. The deeper I dug, the more I realised how much of Barak Valley's legacy, its contributions to the freedom movement, its struggles for linguistic and cultural recognition, and its stories of survival remained undocumented or buried beneath bureaucratic neglect. This book tries to bridge that gap.

A significant part of this effort is reflected in Chapter 23 which compiles essential data on the Members of the Legislative Councils of Eastern Bengal and Assam, Assam Legislative Council, the first Legislative Assembly, and the Central Legislative Council of India. It also documents successive Members of Parliament, key personalities of Barak Valley, including Sufi mystics, and highlights major regional newspapers along with their editors.

This project has been both intellectually challenging and emotionally grounding. I am especially grateful to those who offered oral accounts, narratives not found in books or online, but carried in lived experiences. These voices form the emotional backbone of this work.

This book does not claim to be exhaustive or definitive. Rather, it is an invitation to remember, to question, and to reclaim the past that shaped who we are. I hope it contributes, however modestly, to the ongoing effort to bring Barak Valley's narrative to the national forefront.

Acknowledgements

This book would not have been possible without the unwavering support, guidance, and inspiration of my father, Mamazzad Ahmed Choudhury (Babu). His steady encouragement, deep insights, and patient mentorship guided me at every step of the writing process. I owe him more than words can convey for nurturing my curiosity, sharpening my understanding, and believing in this project from its inception.

I am profoundly indebted to Kamruzzaman Choudhury, an erudite author and a distinguished intellectual force within the Barak Valley, whose scholarly guidance and archival contributions were indispensable to the composition of Chapter 23. His meticulous research and discerning insights into the eminent personages of the Barak Valley, alongside its literary stalwarts, Sufi mystics, and the region's most venerated newspapers and their editorial custodians, have enriched this volume with both depth and authenticity. His intellectual generosity is both acknowledged and deeply appreciated.

A special note of gratitude is reserved for my younger sister, Muazzama Choudhury Fidaa, whose brilliance in the art of language proved to be an unwavering compass throughout this literary voyage. Her mastery of English and her keen editorial eye lent both clarity and elegance to these pages. This book bears not just my name, but the quiet imprint of her intellect and grace, a silent architect behind the words you now read.

I also extend my heartfelt thanks to the people of Barak Valley, whose oral testimonies, shared stories, and lived experiences form the soul of this book. Much of what is recorded here cannot be found in official archives or online, it lives in memory, and I am honoured that so many trusted me with theirs.

Table of Contents

About the Author

Muazzaz Ahmed Choudhury, also known as Faaiz, is a law student, writer, and electronic music producer with various instrumental tracks available on Spotify, JioSaavn, Apple Music, Amazon Music, Shazam, SoundCloud, Boomplay Music, etc. He is also associated with The Rahman Pharmacy, a family-owned medical establishment located at Station Road, Karimganj, Assam with a long-standing legacy of serving the community since the British era. He completed his kindergarten at Tiny Hearts and completed his schooling from Kendriya Vidyalaya Karimganj, Assam. He is the Founder Partner and Management Executive of *'The Capture'* (active from September 2021 to October 2023), a youth-led creative platform that focuses on photography, surveys, and visual storytelling with a commitment to social awareness and cultural expression. *'The Capture'* has garnered attention for its raw, thought-provoking visuals and its dedication to voices from the grassroots. He is a man of his words, with a modern vision and a mind grounded in old-school wisdom.

The author comes from a family rooted in values and service. His father, Mamazzad Ahmed Choudhury (Babu), is an HM at educators field, a researcher, a poet by nature, and a respected community figure known for helping others and resolving disputes with wisdom. He was honoured with the Chishti title at *Ajmer Dargah Sharif*, through the Head Office Ziarat-e-Khwaja, Ajmer Sharif, Rajasthan. A passionate traveller, he has explored North India, Nepal & Bangladesh. The author's mother, Sultana Fahmida Choudhury is a devoted homemaker who has been the emotional backbone of his journey. His younger sister, Muazzama Choudhury Fidaa, with a strong grasp of English, assisted the author in refining parts of this book with clarity and insight well beyond her years.

Faaiz has contributed articles to various platforms:
Youth Ki Awaaz:
•The Education Scam in India: A Growing Concern
•The Indian Budget 2024–25: Falls Short on Equity & Sustainability
•Outrage in Kolkata

Medium:
•From Leaders to Deities: Political Hero Worship in India
•When Homes Become Illegal: The Urban Poor and India's Bulldozer Justice

LinkedIn Articles:
•Civic Sense in India: The Missing Piece in Our Progress
•Brain Drain: Why Indian Students Are Moving Abroad for Higher Education

Faaiz is a descendant of an illustrious family with roots in Mesopotamia and Mughal India. His ancestor, Muhammad Imam Baksh, a prince from Mesopotamia, came to Delhi in 1599 AD to accept the discipleship of the Sufi Hazrat Baqi Billah (R:), in the Nabi Karim area of Delhi, during the reign of Emperor Akbar. His grandson Nawab Jan Muhammad Khan Bahadur was appointed Faujdar of Bihar on 1 Sh'aban, 1074 Hijri/1663 AD (Sanad No.: T997/319) and later in 1666, he was appointed as the Faujdar of Mughal Bengal's Sylhet Sarkar by Emperor Aurangzeb. From their lineage came Dewan Arman Ali Choudhury, the Zamindar of Ujandihi in Karimganj.

During the Partition of 1947, while 111 out of 112 Choudhury families of Ujandihi migrated to East Pakistan (now Bangladesh), his great-grandfather, Dr. Rosman Ali Choudhury, a freedom fighter and reputed British-era physician, chose to stay in India, believing in the principles of democracy and sovereignty. This legacy of service and resilience inspires Faaiz's work.

I

Barak Valley — Assam's Untold Chapter Begins

The Barak Valley, located in the southern part of Assam, is a distinct and richly layered region often overlooked in discussions about the Northeast. Comprising three districts — Cachar, Karimganj, and Hailakandi. it stretches across fertile plains, tea-covered hills, and lush forests, all threaded by the lifeline of the valley: the Barak River.

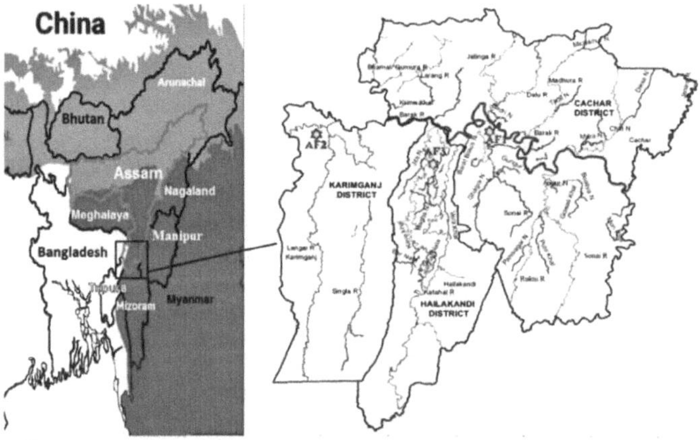

Fig: Map of Barak Valley showing the districts Cachar, Karimganj, and Hailakandi. Modified from Saha and Gupta (2019).

Geographically, the Barak Valley is bordered by Mizoram to the south, Manipur to the east, and Bangladesh to the west. The Cachar district, with Silchar as its headquarters, connects closely with Manipur and Mizoram, while Karimganj shares an international border with Bangladesh and proximity to Tripura through its southwestern frontier. Hailakandi, the central district among the three, borders Mizoram directly on its southern side and serves as a transit corridor between Cachar and the neighbouring state. These boundaries not only define strategic geography but also shape migration, trade, and cultural exchange across the region.

This physical layout gives Barak Valley a unique identity as a gateway, both into the Northeastern hills and out toward the Bangladesh plains, often overlooked in discussions about the Northeast. The Barak River, flowing from Manipur into Assam and eventually splitting into the Surma and Kushiyara rivers in Bangladesh, the Barak River is more than a geographical feature, it is a cultural and emotional artery for millions.

Barak Valley is home to a population exceeding 4 million, with a diverse demographic spread. The majority are Bengali-speaking, particularly in the Sylheti dialect, which is distinct in phonetics, rhythm, and cultural expression. Other communities include Manipuris, Dimasas, Bishnupriyas, Marwaris, Tea Planter Community and tribal groups, making the valley a harmonious mosaic of languages, religions, and customs.

Despite being geographically and culturally integral to Assam, the valley often stands apart in socio-political terms. The literacy rate in Barak Valley stands roughly around 80%, close to the national average, but educational infrastructure is heavily skewed toward Silchar. Institutions like Assam University, Silchar Medical College, and Kendriya Vidyalayas in all three districts cater to thousands, while rural areas still face challenges with access, dropout rates, and digital learning gaps.

The economic profile of Barak Valley is modest. Agriculture, tea cultivation, small-scale trade, and public service form the backbone of the region's income sources. While Karimganj benefits from international trade via Sutarkandi, and Hailakandi from agriculture and rubber plantations, the region lacks major industrial setups. The closure of the Panchgram Paper Mill & Cachar Sugar Mill remains symbolic of lost potential and unfulfilled promises. As a result, many young professionals migrate to Guwahati, Delhi, Mumbai, Chennai, Kolkata, or even the Gulf countries in search of work.

Barak Valley is also a hub of religious and cultural pluralism. In this region, Durga Puja and Eid are celebrated with equal grandeur, and masjids and mandirs stand close to one another, reflecting harmony. Religious events become communal gatherings rather than sources of conflict. Spiritual landmarks like Bishkut Dargah Sharif, Dargah of Hazrat Shah Adam Khaki, Town Kali Bari, St. Thomas Church, Roman Catholic Church and the ISKCON temple in Silchar are not just religious spaces, but sites of shared memory and coexistence.

The valley's terrain, however, presents significant logistical and climatic challenges. Heavy rainfall and frequent landslides in the hilly areas of Cachar and Hailakandi disrupt road and rail transport during monsoon seasons. Flooding along the Barak River routinely displaces families and damages infrastructure. Furthermore, flight connectivity remains limited, with no direct links to cities like Delhi, Mumbai or Bengaluru. The Silchar Airport is modest and often overcrowded, relying heavily on Kolkata for major connections.

The rail network, while improved with broad-gauge conversion, still struggles with frequent delays, and road connectivity remains inadequate with pothole-ridden highways and incomplete bypasses, especially in and around Karimganj. The valley's transport challenges affect not only commerce but also healthcare access, emergency response, and tourism. Despite this, the spirit of Barak's people remains resilient. The valley has produced freedom fighters, scholars, writers, doctors, journalists, and artists who have contributed nationally and internationally. The younger generation is increasingly turning to digital platforms, local journalism, photography, and music production to assert their identity and reclaim representation.

This book is both a tribute and a testimony. It does not attempt to romanticize hardship but rather seeks to illuminate the reality of a region too often left out of Assam's mainstream narrative. Authors, researchers and columnists such as Dr. Tapodhir Bhattacharjee through his essays and academic contributions, have laid early foundations of Barak Valley's literature and history. Local media like Samayik Prasanga, Jugoshonko, Nababarta Prasanga & others continue this legacy in their own way.

Several eminent political figures of Barak Valley have achieved recognition and electoral success beyond the region, representing constituencies outside their native land. Moinul Hoque Choudhury, one of the most prominent leaders from Barak Valley, was elected as the Member of Parliament from Dhubri Parliamentary Constituency in Assam. Barrister A. F. Golam Osmani, another towering personality, served as an elected MP from Barpeta Parliamentary Constituency. Santosh Mohan Dev, a veteran leader from Silchar, was elected from the North Tripura Parliamentary Constituency, reflecting his political influence beyond the valley. Sushmita Dev, daughter of Santosh Mohan Dev, has also made her mark by being elected twice as a Member of Parliament (Rajya Sabha) from West Bengal, symbolizing the growing presence of Barak origin leaders on a national scale. Moreover, Mahmudur Rahman Mazumdar, son of Sarpanch Wajid Ali Mazumdar of Chandinagar, Katigorah, who was born in Chandinagar, became an elected MP from the Kanaighat–Zakiganj Constituency in Bangladesh during the period of 1981-1991, showcasing the historical and cultural ties of Barak Valley with the Sylhet region. Additionally, Triguna Sen, an eminent educationist and former Union Minister, was elected to the Rajya Sabha from the state of Tripura, further highlighting the political reach of Barak-origin leaders.

In the chapters that follow, we will explore the struggles, stories, heritage, movements, faith, and future of Barak Valley. But before that, this introduction stands as a reminder, that Barak Valley is not a fringe, not an afterthought. It is a land with its own identity, its own rhythm, and its own right to be remembered.

Here begins the untold chapter.

II
The Language That We Bled For

"We were told to speak someone else's tongue.
We answered with blood, and silence never returned."

Barak Valley does not speak softly, it speaks Bengali. But that very voice, so central to our identity, once cost our people their lives.

The Bengali Language Movement of 1961 is not just a forgotten page of Assam's history, it is a wound carved into the heart of Barak Valley. A wound that still throbs with pride and pain. A movement not for dominance, but for dignity. Not against a language, but for the right to hold our own.

What Happened in 1961?

After the reorganization of states and rising Assamese nationalism, the Assam Government passed a bill declaring Assamese as the sole official language of the state to be implemented in all official government functions, even in Bengali-majority areas like Barak Valley.

This meant that students, teachers, government employees, lawyers, everyone would have to abandon their mother tongue in their official and professional lives. For a region where more than 80% of the population spoke Bengali or Sylheti, this decision was not just inconvenient. It was an erasure.

The people of Cachar, Karimganj, and Hailakandi protested. peacefully. They wrote petitions. They raised slogans. They organized several meetings and student rallies. And finally, on May 19, 1961, a massive non-violent protest took place at Silchar Railway Station, joined by similar gatherings across the valley, including Karimganj town and rural blocks.

The Martyrs of a Valley

In Silchar, police opened fire without warning. Eleven unarmed protestors died on the spot. Among them were:

- Kamala Bhattacharjee, a teenage girl
- Birendra Sutradhar, a shopkeeper
- Satyendra Deb, a teacher
- Tarani Debnath, a railway employee
- Sunil Sarkar, a student
- Sachindra Chandra Pal, Hitesh Biswas, Kartik Chandra Paul, and others

But Silchar was not alone in its sacrifice.

In Karimganj, several people were also injured and detained for defying state orders. Though the lethal firing happened in Silchar, the martyrs' flame burned across Barak Valley. People from Karimganj also played an essential role in organizing protest meetings, sheltering activists, and keeping the movement alive despite threats.

Many families in Karimganj and Hailakandi still carry memories of that time of student leaders who vanished, of elders who spoke in hushed tones, of Sylheti and Bengali spoken with defiance.

A Movement Written in Blood

This was not just about the Bengali language. It was about a people refusing to be erased.

Many of us who grew up in Barak Valley were raised by those who had lived through that time. Grandparents who whispered these stories in the evening, teachers who made us recite poetry in Sylheti, parents who told us —
"Remember, we didn't inherit this language. We earned it."

They were right. Bengali in Barak is not a state language. It is not a regional convenience. It is a memorial. Every word we speak carries the weight of those who died and those who stood up from Silchar to Karimganj, from

Hailakandi to the smallest village that refused to stay silent.

We bled for the right to speak.
Now, we write for the right to be heard.

"আমার সত্তা" (My Essence)
Written by Mamazzad Ahmed Choudhury, dedicated to the language martyrs on 5th Jaishtha, 1368 Bangla / 19th May 1961:

আমার সত্তা
My Essence

বঙ্গদেশের পাশে থাকি বাংলায় গাহি গান
I stand by Bengal, and sing in Bangla.

বাংলায় কাঁদি আমি বাংলায় বাঁচি প্রাণ।
I weep in Bangla, and my soul thrives in Bangla.

বাংলা আমার সকল সত্তা
Bangla is my entire being.

বাংলা আমার অন্তরাত্মা।
Bangla is my inner soul.

বাংলায় আমি স্বপ্ন দেখি
I dream in Bangla.

বাংলায় আমি কাহিনী লিখি।
I write stories in Bangla.

বাংলায় আমি গর্ব করি বাংলা মম ধ্যান
I take pride in Bangla – it is my meditation.

বাংলায় গানে জুড়ায় দেহ-মন-প্রাণ।
My body, mind, and soul find peace in Bangla songs.

বাংলায় আমি হাসতে জানি
I know how to laugh in Bangla.
বাংলায় আমি মরতে চাহি।
I wish to die in Bangla.

বাংলা আমার মায়ের ভাষা
Bangla is my mother's tongue.

বাংলা আমার মেয়ের ভাষা।
Bangla is my daughter's tongue.
বঙ্গদেশের মাছের ঝোল
The fish curry of Bengal.

জলের মধ্যে ভেটের ফুল।
The water flowers (vet'er phool) in the pond.

বঙ্গনারীর অঙ্গা শোভা
The beauty of the Bengali woman's attire.

খোঁপার মধ্যে চাঁপা গুঁজা।
A champa flower tucked in her hair bun.

সরোবরে শাপলা ফুল
Water lilies in the lake.

আমবাগানে আম্রমুকুল।
Mango buds in the mango orchard.

জারি, শারি বাউলের গান
Jari, Shari, and Baul folk songs.

সিরাজ লালনের অনেক মান।
The glory of Siraj and Lalon lives on.

বঙ্গদেশের নকশি কাঁথা
Bengal's embroidered Nakshi Kantha (quilt).

বীর সেনানীর অমর কথা।
Tales of immortal brave warriors.

বাংলা কাব্য রসে ভরা
Bangla is rich with poetic essence.

বাংলার চর পলি ভরা।
The river islands (chars) of Bengal are fertile with silt.

বাংলার পৌষ পার্বন, বাংলার নবান্ন সিদ্ধপুলি-পাঠীসাপ্টা, সবশেষে মিষ্টান্ন ||
Bengal's Poush festival, Bengal's Nabanna — with siddha puli, pathi sapta, and ending with sweet desserts.

III
Barak During The Liberation - Stories From The Borderline

"The seeds of 1971 were sown in 1947."

In 1971, as the soil of East Pakistan cracked under the weight of revolution, and cries for freedom echoed through the plains of Bengal, the Barak Valley stood still. Yet within that stillness, there was movement of people, of pain, of shared memory. Barak Valley, and particularly Karimganj, stood as a silent yet active front of empathy. This chapter aims not only to retell the events of the Bangladesh Liberation War but to present how an ignored region became a humanitarian corridor.

The Partition of India, shaped overwhelmingly by religion and the desire for a Hindu India and Muslim Pakistan, carved not just geography but emotions. Sylhet, a Bengali Muslim-majority district, was given a referendum, and it voted to merge with East Pakistan (later Bangladesh). But what was overlooked, and forever scarred, was Barak Valley, especially Karimganj, a part of Sylhet that remained in India due to the flow of the Kushiyara River. While politicians were drawing lines on maps, no one thought about the people who shared a language, a culture, and in many cases, families. Barak Valley was left to float in a cultural in-between, a Bengali-speaking, Sylheti-rooted society now separated from its ancestral land. The cultural trauma of that decision haunted the valley for decades, culminating in its silent but powerful role in 1971.

By March 1971, tension in East Pakistan erupted into violence. Operation Searchlight, ordered by the Pakistani military, aimed to crush Bengali nationalism. In retaliation, resistance groups like the Mukti Bahini were formed. The genocide of Bengali intellectuals, students, and civilians began. Various areas of Karimganj town, suburb areas, Ramkrishna Nagar, and surrounding villages were among the first Indian lands to see the influx of refugees. It wasn't just numbers, it was people, hungry, barefoot, clutching children and old memories. Some came by land. Others came by boat, crossing rivers under the moon.

While Delhi debated and Dhaka burned, the boatmen of the Kushiyara River were ferrying life itself. The rivers, usually means of trade and fishing, became routes of rescue. Fishermen in Karimganj navigated through marshy, mined, and military-patrolled waters to help people escape. It wasn't an operation. It was a quiet revolution of humanity. They were never named. But survivors remember their faces. A man with a gamchha[1] tied to his forehead. A boy barely eighteen rowing women to safety. A mother who handed over her infant to strangers on a boat, trusting fate more than soldiers.

When families arrived in Karimganj, many had nowhere to go. But they were not abandoned. Religious spaces, temples, churches, mosques across Karimganj, Silchar, and Hailakandi functioned not as doctrines, but as dwellings.

In Hailakandi, many frontline female volunteered to run a makeshift clinic with limited medicine and no electricity. Other women cooked for weeks in community kitchens. Dr. Rosman Ali Choudhury, already a senior physician and a freedom fighter of British India, treated the wounded. He refused government recognition, saying: *"This is not help. This is duty."*

---

[1] A traditional cotton towel.

In makeshift shelters, women formed counseling circles. They taught children songs, gave girls a comb and dignity, and whispered prayers into sleeping ears.

The 1971 Bangladesh Liberation War is remembered for its heroes, its revolution, its creation of a new nation. But Barak Valley remained unacknowledged. There were no headlines. No monuments. But in every refugee who survived, in every rescued child, in every silent mother who lit a fire in a stranger's courtyard, Barak lives on. The partition ignored their voice. The liberation echoed it.

Today, the border areas still hum with memory. Sutarkandi, now a trading point, once held screams and silence. Karimganj Railway Station, which saw trains full of the displaced, still stands. Barak's contribution was not made in guns and flags, but in compassion, shelter, and spirit. The valley did not choose its border. But it chose its humanity. And perhaps, that's the highest form of revolution.

Beyond the events and statistics, the emotional narrative of Barak Valley during 1971 is written into the soil. Families still talk about the cousins who disappeared, the aunts who never came back, and the brothers who settled across the new border. For many, the war was not a national event but a deeply personal fracture of family. The price was paid in identity, in memories, in a constant ache of displacement. The people of Barak did not see the war as someone else's tragedy. They treated it as their own.

Reports from the time reveal that over 10 million refugees fled to India during the war. Assam, and especially Barak Valley, bore a significant burden. Karimganj alone saw nearly 500,000 refugees pass through in waves. Despite limited infrastructure, the people came together in an unprecedented spirit of collective care.

Among these refugees were poets, singers, and scholars who contributed to Barak's intellectual and cultural vibrancy. Some stayed back. They started new lives in towns Karimganj, Ramkrishna Nagar, Badarpur . Their children became part of the Barak story.

Even decades later, during family gatherings and village fairs, old songs are sung about that time. Not of war, but of kindness. Not of loss, but of refuge. The war, for Barak, was a reminder that while maps may divide, humanity can still unite.

Barak Valley never sought formal recognition for its role. It did not ask for it. Yet, it deserves to be remembered-remembered not just for what it endured, but for what it stood for. This valley opened its doors when the world closed them. It offered refuge when others turned their backs. It spoke a language of mercy and humanity when the louder voices of the time shouted only of power and division.

Barak Valley chose people over politics, compassion over convenience, and action over silence. It became a sanctuary for the forgotten and a beacon for those who believed that kindness still had a place in a fractured world.

Let us remember the heroes whose names were never recorded in history books, those who worked quietly, with no expectation of reward or recognition.

And let us continue to speak for a valley that chose to act when others turned away, so that its story of courage and heart will never be lost to time.

IV
Living Between Borders

"We were not divided by swords.
We were divided by silence."

A Valley of Borders

Barak Valley is a part of Assam. But if you ask most Barakis, it doesn't always feel that way.

We live inside borders: administrative borders, linguistic borders, mental borders, and sometimes even emotional borders.

We are Bengali-speaking people in a state that largely associates its identity with the Assamese language. Our food, festivals, dialects, and even our mourning songs are different. And while diversity should be a strength, it has often been used to other us.

Partition and Psychological Displacement

Barak Valley's identity crisis began long before modern politics. It started with Partition in 1947. When Sylhet was separated from Assam and merged into East Pakistan after a controversial referendum, Barak Valley once part of a cultural whole was cut off from its own soul. Only Karimganj, Hailakandi, and Cachar remained in India. And that too, not as part of Bengal, but as part of Assam.

It was not a crime. It was a compromise.
But compromises, over time, start to feel like corrections we didn't agree to.

Panchgram Paper Mill – A Silent Collapse

There was a time when Barak Valley produced paper for all of Northeast India. That time is now a memory. The Cachar Paper Mill in Panchgram, run by the Hindustan Paper Corporation, was once the pride of the valley. It provided direct employment to 1,500 workers and supported an entire ecosystem of local businesses, schools, and families.

But in October 2015, the mill was shut down due to government mismanagement and unpaid dues. Workers were left without salary for over 50 months. Some died of poverty. Some died by suicide. Others are still fighting not for compensation, but for basic human dignity.

Not only was the Paper Mill shut down, but with its closure, an entire ecosystem crumbled, the surrounding locality lost its heartbeat, and Kendriya Vidyalaya Panchgram, once alive with students and school bells, fell into stillness. The mill had been more than just an industry; it was the foundation upon which daily life stood. Former students of KV Panchgram still recall their school days with warmth and longing, remembering a time when the town thrived with purpose and energy.

Today, those memories live on in quiet reflections, as Panchgram stands as a reminder of a once-vibrant chapter now paused in time.

And yet, this tragedy found no serious coverage in national media. Even within Assam, it became a political talking point, not a human story. Panchgram didn't just shut down a mill. It shut down the hopes of an entire generation in Barak.

Cachar Sugar Mill – Collapse of Barak Valley's Industrial Dream

The Cachar Sugar Mill, located in Basattihal, Ratabari, Karimganj district, was once the pride of Barak Valley's industrial landscape. Established in 1976, with the aim of promoting agro-based industry and generating employment, the mill played a vital role in the region's economic aspirations. Its foundation was part of a broader developmental vision supported by regional leaders such as Moinul Haque Mazumdar, who advocated for infrastructural and industrial growth in South Assam.

However, the mill's journey from promise to failure was marked by systemic mismanagement, financial losses, corruption, and a decline in sugarcane cultivation. Despite its socio-economic importance, successive governments failed to revive it effectively. By the early 2000s, the mill was shut down, leaving behind shattered livelihoods and an abandoned industrial complex.

The collapse of Cachar Sugar Mill represents more than the failure of one factory, it signifies the death of Barak Valley's early industrial hopes and a long-standing neglect of regional development. Today, its ruins stand as a stark reminder of what could have been, had vision been matched with commitment and governance.

A Generation in Waiting

The youth of Barak are educated, ambitious, and capable. But opportunity here is scarce.

- There are no major industries apart from tea and a few small-scale sectors.
- Government jobs are few and far between.
- Private sector presence is almost non-existent.
- Startups and tech parks that are blooming in other parts of Assam barely touch Barak.

Most students are forced to migrate to Guwahati, Kolkata, Delhi or Bengaluru leaving behind their parents, heritage, and soil. Those who stay often work in temporary coaching centres, contractual teaching, or petty commerce, always waiting for something more.

The Struggle for Representation

Even in politics, Barak Valley often feels like an afterthought. Despite having multiple MLAs and MPs, decisions that affect this region are often made without regional consultation. Important demands like restoring the paper mill, improving infrastructure, preserving Sylheti heritage, or increasing college funding rarely reach the top.

Despite all the challenges, Barak Valley has not given up.
Our poets still write.
Our students still dream.
Our people still vote, not because they trust, but because they believe.

V
Faith, Family & Coexistence

"আমি চিরদিন অবমানিতের পাশে,
আমি চিরদিন বেদনার, দুঃখের, ভবিষ্যতের কণ্ঠস্বর।
আমি হিন্দু, আমি মুসলমান,
আমি শিখ, আমি খ্রিস্টান— আমি ক্রীতদাসের স্বাধীনতা!"

"I have always stood with the insulted.
I am the voice of sorrow, pain, and tomorrow.
I am Hindu, I am Muslim,
I am Sikh, I am Christian — I am the freedom of the enslaved!"
— Inspired by Kazi Nazrul Islam

A Valley of Many Faiths

In a country often fractured by religious divisions, Barak Valley stands out as a rare example of peaceful coexistence. Here, you'll find a Hindu home that sends sweets to its Muslim neighbours during Eid, and a Muslim carpenter building a Durga pandal with equal devotion. In the same lane, one might hear the azaan floating over rooftops just moments before a conch shell sounds from a puja room. Unlike in many parts of India, religion in Barak Valley is not a political identity, it is a personal faith. Communities don't live in silos. They live in shared spaces, with shared languages, shared grief, and shared joys.

Notably, Barak Valley also remains one of the few regions in India where casteism plays little to no role in public or private life. While surnames and ancestral backgrounds are known, social discrimination based on caste is rare, especially in urban and semi-urban spaces. Interactions in schools, markets, workplaces, and neighbourhoods reflect a deep rooted cultural equality, where people are judged more by their character than their caste.

This absence of caste hierarchy has allowed Barak Valley to nurture a more inclusive society, where community bonds are based on trust, not tradition.

Interfaith Relations – Rooted in Mutual Respect

The reason this harmony survives is not because we are perfect but because we are practical and emotionally connected. In Karimganj, Silchar, and Hailakandi, Muslim shopkeepers are often seen donating to local Kali Puja committees. In return, Hindu and Christian communities contribute to Eid feasts, Muharram processions, or mosque repairs. No matter what religion they follow, everyone enjoys eating jalebis from *Devdoot* during the month of Ramzan.

Marriages may not always cross religious lines, but friendships, businesses, cultural events, and everyday life do. What unites Barak's people is not just tolerance, but affection a sense that we may pray differently, but we hurt and heal the same way.

Shared Culture Beyond Religion

Whether it's Mahalaya songs on the radio, Nazrul Geeti at school functions, or the taste of Hilsa Fish with Mustard Seed (Shoishyo er Elish) at a Muslim wedding, religion rarely acts as a cultural boundary in Barak.

Language: Most people, regardless of religion, speak either Bengali or Sylheti, laugh at the same proverbs, and use the same nicknames: mama, dada, apa, didi.

Food: From panta bhaat to shutki maas, food unites households across faiths.

Festivals: You'll often see Muslims attending Durga Puja melas, and Hindus visiting Sufi shrines during urs.

Songs: Both Hindu and Muslim families sing the same Sylheti folk tunes, sometimes in weddings, sometimes in grief.

When Tensions Arise — Silence or Strength?

Yes, Barak is not free from the occasional ripple of communal tension, especially when political narratives from outside try to enter and divide.

But unlike cities where mob violence erupts quickly, Barak's people usually hold the line.

Instead of riots, there are dialogues.

Instead of threats, there are temples and mosques requesting calm together.

Instead of revenge, there is remembrance of who we are as neighbours.

The elders often say:

"আমরা একই ধানক্ষেত থেকে খাই।
আমরা কীভাবে এটিকে যুদ্ধক্ষেত্রে পরিণত করতে পারি?"
"We eat from the same rice field.
How can we turn it into a battlefield ?"

We, the people of Barak Valley, have always lived in harmony, embracing our diversity with pride and respect. Whether Hindu, Muslim, Christian, or of any other faith, we share the same streets, celebrate each other's festivals, and stand by one another in times of joy and struggle. We will never allow anyone to sow seeds of hatred or discrimination among us. Our unity is our greatest strength, and we are determined to preserve it. No political force or divisive agenda can break the deep rooted bond that connects us. Barak Valley is not just a region, it is a living example of peaceful coexistence, and we, its people, will always protect it.

As Guru Nanak said:

"Before becoming A Muslim,
A Sikh, A Hindu, or A Christian
Let's become Human first"

The Role of Family & Local Leadership

Barak Valley's peaceful and pluralistic fabric is deeply interwoven with the strength of its families and the wisdom of its grassroots leadership. In this culturally diverse region, home to Hindus, Muslims, Christians, Sikhs, and various indigenous communities, peace is not maintained merely by law, but by living traditions passed down in households and upheld in neighborhoods.

From an early age, children are taught values that transcend religion and politics. In homes across the valley, whether in a Muslim village near Badarpur or a Hindu locality in Silchar, young ones are reminded to:

- Greet elders of all communities with equal respect
- Never insult or mock another's deity or sacred rituals
- Celebrate Eid, Diwali, Bihu, and Christmas not just as observers, but as neighbours
- Choose friends by the warmth of their hearts, not the language of their prayers

These teachings are not just moral guidelines, they are acts of everyday resistance against communalism.

At times of unrest or political tension, it is not uncommon to see local imams, temple priests, pastors, community elders, and political leaders across parties joining hands to uphold harmony. In border towns like Karimganj or the mixed lanes of Hailakandi, when provocations have threatened to polarize, it is often the peace committees, madrassa teachers, school principals, and retired elders who come forward to mediate, not with force, but with wisdom, empathy, and history as their guide.

Their interventions are deeply rooted in a shared memory, that the Barak Valley has always been a land of coexistence. These leaders remind their people not of what divides them, but of what binds them: a common river, a shared tea garden, a neighbour's helping hand, or a childhood spent playing together across religious lines.

In a world increasingly torn by hate and echo chambers, Barak's model of local peace-building offers a quiet but powerful lesson: when families nurture respect and leaders choose unity over division, even the most diverse societies can live in harmony.

VI
The Sylheti Legacy

"আমি সিলেটি, আমি বাংলার ঢেউয়ে জন্মানো একটি অনুরণন।"
"I am Sylheti, an echo born of Bengal's waves."

The soul of Barak Valley speaks softly in a voice called Sylheti, a language that defines the very heartbeat of Cachar, Hailakandi, and Karimganj. Sylheti is not a borrowed dialect or a cultural leftover from Sylhet in present-day Bangladesh. It is the mother tongue of the people of Barak, spoken in every corner of this valley with passion, pride, and poetry.

A Language Born from Barak's Earth

Though linguistically close to Bengali, Sylheti stands apart with its unique vocabulary, phonetic features, and oral traditions. It has historically had its own script, the Sylheti Nagri and thrives in songs, lullabies, jokes, and folk narratives. In Barak Valley, Sylheti is not just a means of communication, it is an emotional identity passed down generations.

From the bazaars of Silchar to the ghats of Karimganj, from the rice fields of Hailakandi to the classrooms and college corridors, Sylheti continues to flow freely. It shapes how we think, how we feel, how we connect with each other. It is a language that has never bowed to erasure, even when officialdom tried to dismiss it as "just a dialect."

An Identity of Resilience

The Sylheti-speaking population of Barak Valley never had to reclaim their roots, they never lost them. Even after the partition of India in 1947, when Sylhet was divided and much of it became a part of East Pakistan (now Bangladesh), the people of Barak, who already belonged to this land, remained firm in identity and culture.

Among the most distinguished lineages of Barak is that of Zamindar Dewan Arman Ali Choudhury of Ujandihi, whose ancestors trace back to Mesopotamia. It begins with Yar Ali Sultan, a nobleman of Mesopotamian origin, who served as a Governor of Farah, Khorasan, during the reign of Shah Tahmasp I (1524–1576). At that time, it was a common imperial policy not to appoint local men as governors in their own homelands, both to prevent the rise of regional loyalties and to strengthen centralized authority. Accordingly, Yar Ali Sultan, hailing from the heartlands of Mesopotamia, was appointed Governor of Khorasan, a vast and strategically crucial eastern province known for its spiritual centres and military significance. His position was not only one of prestige but also of delicate trust, reflecting the Safavid court's reliance on capable men of foreign origin to administer its frontier provinces.

Shah Tahmasp I, under whom Yar Ali Sultan served, was no ordinary monarch. He was the same Persian king who, in an extraordinary moment of imperial diplomacy, granted asylum and military support to the exiled Mughal Emperor Humayun. This historic act of refuge ensured Humayun's eventual restoration to the throne of Delhi and laid the groundwork for enduring cultural, diplomatic, and intellectual exchange between Safavid Persia and Mughal India. These ties were more than political; they were familial, ideological, and spiritual, and through the bloodline of Yar Ali Sultan, they would eventually run deep into the soil of Bengal.

Note that, Iraq is famous throughout the world for Mesopotamia, the world's oldest civilization. This civilization developed around 6,000 BC around the Tigris and Euphrates rivers. It included parts of the present-day Arab world, including Iran, Kuwait, Turkey, Syria, and Jordan. Mesopotamia is a historical region of West Asia situated within the Tigris-Euphrates river system, in the northern part of the Fertile Crescent. Today, Mesopotamia is known as present-day Iraq and forms the eastern geographic boundary of the modern Middle East. Just beyond it lies southwestern Iran, where the region transitions into the Persian plateau, marking the shift from the Arab world to Iran. In the broader sense, the historical region of Mesopotamia also includes parts of present-day Iran (southwest), Turkey (southeast), Syria (northeast), and Kuwait.

Yar Ali Sultan's legacy continued through his son, Prince Muhammad Imam Baksh, a devout scholar, who came to Delhi in 1599 AD to accept the discipleship of the Sufi saint Hazrat Baqi Billah (R:), the pioneer of the Naqshbandi Sufi Order in the Indian subcontinent, in the Nabi Karim area of Delhi, during Emperor Akbar's reign.

Prince Jahangir got to know Prince Muhammad Imam Baksh, because Prince Jahangir often came to the service of Hazrat Baqi Billah (R:). After the death of Hazrat Baqi Billah (R:), Prince Muhammad Imam Baksh managed the activities of Khaneka Sharif. Later Emperor Jahangir ascended the throne in 1605 AD, and Muhammad Imam Baksh was welcomed into the Mughal court due to his royal bloodline. After staying at the hospitality of Emperor for a few days, Emperor Jahangir appointed him to the royal office due to his being a member of the royal family of Mesopotamia. He managed the royal office for a long time with great skill and found a cosmopolitan court where scholars, administrators, and nobles from the Safavid realm were welcomed into the Mughal fold. His journey marked not just migration, but a continuation of an imperial and spiritual alliance between the two empires. Later settled in the modern Nabi Karim area of Delhi. He and his wife's tombs are located next to the shrine of Hazrat Baqi Billah (R:).

His son, Nawab Aqil Khan also known as Mir Muhammad Askari, inherited not only noble descent but also martial prowess. During the reign of Shah Jahan (1628–1658), he served as an officer in the Wala Shahi Household of Mughal Army, a prominent position in Burhanpur under the Mughals, and he was also given charge of Ilkandal (Elgandal), which was a dependency of Hyderabad. His rise through the ranks was grounded in both battlefield distinction and administrative capability.
Nawab Aqil Khan had four sons, namely, the learned Dewan Dween Muhammad, Nawab Jan Muhammad Khan Bahadur, Dewan Jamal Muhammad and Dewan Kamal Muhammad.

Among them, Nawab Jan Muhammad Khan Bahadur, also known as Nur-ud-Din Muhammad, the second son of Nawab Aqil Khan, emerged as a prominent figure. After serving in various capacities in the Mughal army, was appointed as the Faujdar of Bihar by Mughal Emperor Aurangzeb, Sanad No. T-997/319 on 1Shaban, 1074 AH/1663 AD. In 1666, he became the Faujdar of Srihatta (Sylhet). The post of Faujdar was one of considerable power, conferring both civil and military authority over a significant region. His brothers also held significant administrative posts under the Mughal darbar, contributing to the foundation of revenue systems in the eastern frontier of Bengal.

After his administrative service in Sylhet, Jan Muhammad Khan Bahadur returned to Burhanpur, as it was Mughal stronghold of political and military importance, served as the Deccan headquarters of Mughals until Aurangzeb moved the capital to Aurangabad.

Jan Muhammad Khan Bahadur was succeeded by his notable sons – Nawab Shuja Ud-din Muhammad Khan, Muhammad Anar Khan and Muhammad Mucha Raja Khan.

In later years, Nawab Jan Muhammad Khan Bahadur, the learned Dewan Dween Mohammad, Dewan Jamal Mohammad and Dewan Kamal Mohammad, impressed by the wisdom of their four brothers and in accordance with the duties given by the Mughal Emperor, Jan Muhammad and his three brothers arrived by River Kushiyara in the Karimganj area of the Srihatta region of East Bengal with the intention of establishing permanent settlement and thus settled *Dihi*[2], that is, in the present-day Chandsrikona on the banks of the Kushiyara river. According to legend, after reaching this place, it was time for the moon to set, the time for the obligatory prayer was approaching, so orders were given to anchor the huge boats for the companions to offer prayers, from that time the place was known as Chanddihi. Later, it was named Chandsrikona. After staying there for a few days, as this place seemed uninhabitable, they sailed upstream again, i.e. against the current, he established a settlement in the present-day Greater Karnamadhu. By sailing upstream along the, Noti Khal the Naughty Canal, which connects the Longai River to the present-day Karimganj city. Jan Muhammad Khan Bahadur named the place where they sailed upstream and established a dihi, Ujan-dihi.

The canal connecting the Kushiyara and Longai rivers is an attraction in Karimganj city. Various goods were brought from different parts of East Bengal and anchored there. During the British period, a bridge was built on this canal, which flowed on the Kushiyara stream, in the 1920s. This bridge was named Earl's Bridge after Earl Saheb, an engineer of the Public Works Department of Sylhet. Over time, the junction of the Naughty Canal with the Kushiyara river, the source of the river, was filled in. It is believed that Noti Khal was blocked at the mouth of its

---

[2]Administrative & Revenue Collection Centre; Tehsil office of the Zamindar.

junction with Kushiyara as a measure to save the town from flooding.

The Zamindari of Nawab Jan Muhammad Khan Bahadur and his fraternity extended from Ujandihi-Bishkut to Shahbazpur in the west and the borders of the Balaut Zamindari in the north in East Bengal.

An "establishment of rural settlement" named Janpur was founded in the name of Nawab Jan Muhammad Khan Bahadur, on the banks of the Longai River adjacent to Karimganj town.
Another village named Kamalpur was established north of village Bishkut in the name of the fourth brother Dewan Kamal Muhammad. Apart from this, the taluks were named Anarpur after his son, Muhammad Anar Khan, Keshar Kapan after grandson Muhammad Keshar Khan, and Chandpur was named after Chand Muhammad Khan.

His son, Shuja-Ud-Din Muhammad Khan would rise to become one of the most powerful men in eastern India. Appointed Faujdar of Sylhet in 1719. He received support from Mughal Emperor, Muhammad Shah in Delhi, who was ready to help him and thus, he ascended to the post of Nawab of Bengal in 1727, ruling until 1739. His governance brought stability and economic growth, and he is remembered as a pragmatic and influential statesman of the late Mughal era. Siyar-ul-Mutakherin by Mir Gholam Hussein Khan Tabtabai (translated into English by Lieutenant Colonel John Briggs, M.R.A.S., The British East India Company (Madras Army) in May, 1831) notes that the reign of Nawab Shuja-Dd-Din Muhammad was one of the best 12 years of the 18th century for the Subah of Bengal. Well known to be a mild, just, secular and God fearing person. Shuja was always interested in learning, jurisprudence and meeting new people who visited Murshidabad from other parts of the world. He was an able administrator and was tactful in dealing with the

Mughal Emperor, Nawab of Oudh, Marathas, East India Company, his ambitious Nazims, ensured proper checks, balances and controls. He was vastly popular among his subjects as well as with the Mughal Emperor Muhammad Shah.

Shuja Ud-Din died on August 26, 1739 and buried in Roshnibag in Murshidabad, leaving behind two sons – Sarfaraz Khan (Nawab of Bengal, Bihar and Orissa) & Muhammad Taqi (Naib Nazim[3] of Orissa) and two daughters, one of whom was married to Mirza Lutfullah Khan Tabrizi (Naib Nazim of Jahangirnagar, Dacca[4] and later Orissa).

However, the path of his brother Muhammad Anar Khan from whom this family directly descends, took a markedly different turn.

Rather than follow the road of power, his brother chose the path of spirituality, embracing a quiet life in Ujandihi, focused on Sufi contemplation and community leadership. Though born into a family of warriors and governors, he chose instead to cultivate a legacy rooted in ethics, devotion, and local service. Over the next two centuries, this branch of the family became pillars of regional leadership under British rule, gradually taking on roles in local governance and land administration. By the 19th century, they had acquired the hereditary title of Dewan, signifying their importance in managing land revenue and upholding regional order.

This noble line continued through Muhammad Keshar Khan, followed by Muhammad Ali Khan, later Dewan

---

[3] A Deputy or Sub-Governor, acting on behalf of the Nazim (Governor)

[4] Presently Dhaka

Chadir Choudhury, then, Dewan Arman Ali Choudhury, and then, Dr. Rosman Ali Choudhury.

Muhammad Ali Khan had two sons – Dewan Muhammad Chadir Choudhury and Muhammad Hachir Choudhury.

Dewan Muhammad Chadir Choudhury had donated a large amount of land for various religious institutions – Karnamadhu-Bishkut Idgah, graveyards, roads and charitable works in this region. He had two sons Dewan Arman Ali Choudhury and Moulvi Forman Ali Choudhury.

The ancient and aesthetically impressive residence of Dewan Muhammad Chadir Choudhury was located on the right side of the road leading to Bishkut village, extending all the way to Kamalpur, a seven-stepped residence. In front of the house, to the north, lay a large and scenic pond that added to the grandeur of the estate. However, an unusual situation arose over time. During daylight hours, tigers were frequently seen roaming the courtyard, creating a sense of insecurity for the family. As a result, Dewan Muhammad Chadir Choudhury took the decision to construct a new residence at a safer location and relocated the family surrounded by his rayats[5].

The fifth generation of Nawab Jan Muhammad Khan Bahadur was Dewan Arman Ali Choudhury, the Zamindar of Ujandihi who had provided the settlement of the land of Ayla Bari Tea Estate to the Eastern Commercial Tea Company. In addition, he was the main patron and land donor of Bishkut Saheb Bari and Ujandihi Saheb Bari. He had three sons – Ajmal Ali Choudhury, Akmal Ali Choudhury and Dr. Rosman Ali Choudhury.

---

[5] Rayat (rai'ot) - a subject/tenant farmer or peasant who cultivates land and other duties vested upon him in zamindari system.

The youngest son of Dewan Arman Ali Choudhury was the renowned physician Dr. Rosman Ali Choudhury, born in December 1902. After passing the entrance examination from Karimganj Government Boys High School, he diligently enrolled in Berry White School of Medicine, Dibrugarh (presently Assam Medical College and Hospital, and obtained a degree in medical science on 22nd June 1921 during the British rule. Later, he joined the Health Department of the British government. He provided health services with a good reputation. Throughout his life, he served in various hospitals in different parts of Assam, especially Balipara Frontier Tract, Tezpur, North-East Frontier Agency (NEFA), East Bengal and the present Civil Hospital run by the then Local Board in Karimganj. People in Karimganj town addressed him as *Munshi Saheb*.

He was a freedom fighter. He actively participated in the freedom movement. But, he refused to accept the freedom fighter's pension, believing that his contribution to India's independence was his duty, not a job.

He once said,

"আমার জাতিকে দাসত্ব থেকে মুক্ত করবার জন্য কোনো পারিশ্রমিক গ্রহণ করি না।"

("I do not accept any wage for liberating my nation from the chains of bondage.")

Ujandihi, an elite residential area known for its cultural refinement. Out of the 112 Choudhury families in Ujandihi at the time of partition, only one — Dr. Rosman Ali Choudhury's family, chose to remain in India while the rest migrated to East Pakistan now Bangladesh.

During the partition of the country in 1947 and in the following few years, 111 elite families, who were granted Choudhury title bestowed by the Mughal emperor upon individuals of notable sttus and influence, related to land ownership and administrative roles, settled in various places in the Sylhet region of present-day Bangladesh and were appointed to various important positions in the government of that time based on their educational qualifications merit and efficiency. But many could not accept the idea of leaving the place of birth for which they had fought for the independence of the country and leaving their homeland in this way. This is evident from the long sighs of many. The uprooted families may have made considerable progress economically. But their peace of mind has undoubtedly declined. There was no communal or political reason behind leaving the estate in this way, but the social reason was the civil unrest and rayat revolt and the abolition of zamindari system in India, primarily enacted in 1950.

A government primary educational institution named 870 No. Choudhury Rosman Ali Primary School was established in his name at Karnamadhu, Karimganj District of Assam.

Dr. Rosman Ali Choudhury was married to Akhtarun Nessa Choudhury, daughter of Amin Ali Choudhury, Zamindar of Bishkut and had three sons and three daughters, namely, Moshud Ahmed Choudhury, Nazir

Ahmed Choudhury, Jahir Ahmed Choudhury, Suraiya Chowdhury, Razia Choudhury and Rabeya Choudhury.

His eldest son, Mashud Ahmed Choudhury, also passed his degree in Pharmacology from Assam Medical College, Dibrugarh and served first at Silchar Civil Hospital and later as Chief Matron at Silchar Medical College & Hospital, Assam.

His eldest daughter Suraiya Chowdhury, was the wife of Engineer Monwar Ali Chowdhury, who was the DivisionalTelecommunication Engineer of Railway Deptt., first in Calcutta, West Bengal and later in Chittagong, East Bengal, whose elder brother, Dr. Sunawar Ali Chowdhury, was the General Manager of Bangladesh Railways. She currently lives in New York, USA.

The second daughter, Razia Choudhury, was the wife of Mahbubur Rahman, a renowned advocate of Karimganj, who was the founder-principal of Karimganj Law College. Her son Jafar Md. Azizul Karim Tapadar, AJS serving as Civil Judge (Senior Division) cum Asstt. Session Judge.

The youngest daughter, Rabeya Choudhury, was the wife of former Minister and five-time member of the Assam Legislative Assembly, Advocate Abdul Muqtadir Choudhury. It is worth noting that Abdul Muqtadir Choudhury's father was Khan Bahadur Abdul Majid Choudhury, who was also a member of the Assam Legislative Assembly in 1937.

Dr. Choudhury's youngest son, Jahir Ahmed Choudhury, was a mechanical engineer and government registered contractor and supplier. He was involved in various social activities and establishments.

Dr. Rosman Ali Choudhury's second son was Nazir Ahmed Choudhury, an eminent personality of Karimganj town. After completing schooling from Karimganj Government Higher Secondary School, obtained degree in Pharmacology from Assam Medical College, Dibrugarh and served in Govt. hospitals at Cachar and Karimganj Civil Hospital. Later in 1958, he joined his father's pharamacetical establishment – The Rahman Pharmacy, a renowned establishment on Station Road, Karimganj, originally founded by his father during the British era and served the people with a lifetime of reputation with skill and competence, according to his qualifications. Married to Jakia Aktar Choudhury of Bagbari, daughter of eminent scholar Abdul Munim Choudhury, former Member of Legislative Assembly and have four sons and one daughter, namely Mamazzad Ahmed Choudhury, Shahadat Ahmed Choudhury, Safat Ahmed Choudhury, Muzakkir Ahmed Choudhury & Choudhury Simin Aktar.

Mamazzad Ahmed Choudhury is an educator, researcher, poet, social worker and writer. He is the Executive Trustee of Bishkut Dargah Preservation and Development Trust, Secretary General of Karnamadhu-Bishkut Idgah Committee, Secretary of Bishkut Dargah Sharif Madrassa and Research Centre. And, involved with various non-governmental organizations. He has one son and one daughter, Muazzaz Ahmed Choudhury (Faaiz) and Muazzama Choudhury Fidaa.

Their collective contributions extended beyond medicine and law to public service, engineering, commerce, and education.

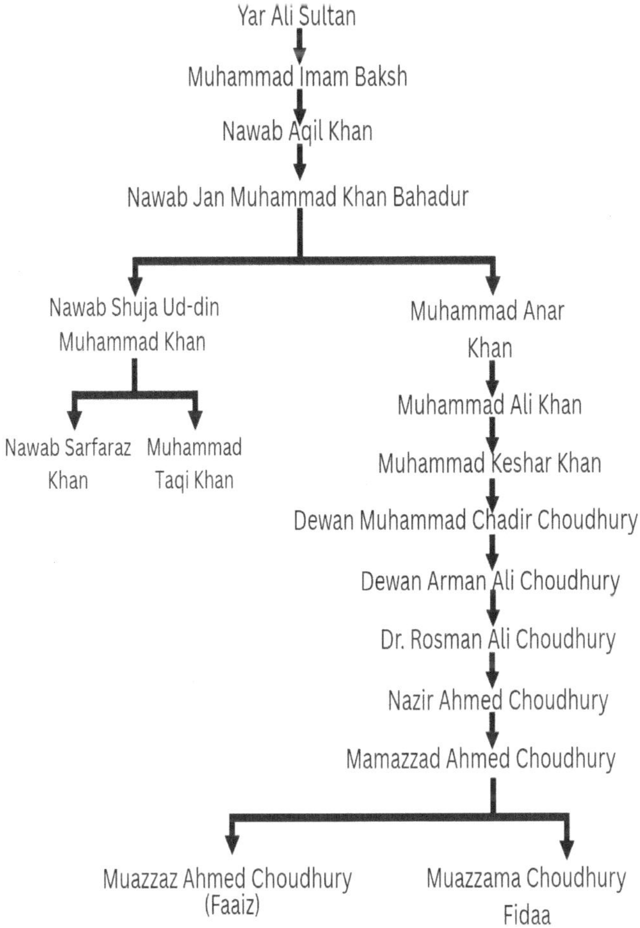
Yar Ali Sultan
Muhammad Imam Baksh
Nawab Aqil Khan
Nawab Jan Muhammad Khan Bahadur
Nawab Shuja Ud-din Muhammad Khan
Muhammad Anar Khan
Nawab Sarfaraz Khan
Muhammad Taqi Khan
Muhammad Ali Khan
Muhammad Keshar Khan
Dewan Muhammad Chadir Choudhury
Dewan Arman Ali Choudhury
Dr. Rosman Ali Choudhury
Nazir Ahmed Choudhury
Mamazzad Ahmed Choudhury
Muazzaz Ahmed Choudhury (Faaiz)
Muazzama Choudhury Fidaa

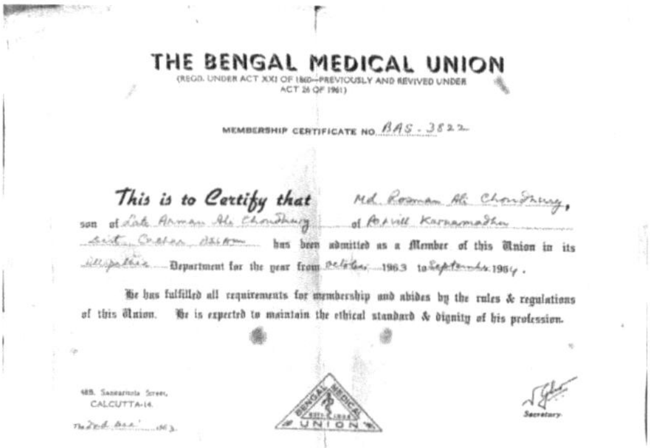

THE BENGAL MEDICAL UNION
(REGD. UNDER ACT XXI OF 1860—PREVIOUSLY AND REVIVED UNDER ACT 26 OF 1961)

MEMBERSHIP CERTIFICATE NO. BAS-3822

This is to Certify that Md. Rosman Ali Choudhury, son of Late Arman Ali Choudhury of ... Karnamadhu ... Assam has been admitted as a Member of this Union in its Allopathic Department for the year from October 1963 to September 1964.

He has fulfilled all requirements for membership and abides by the rules & regulations of this Union. He is expected to maintain the ethical standard & dignity of his profession.

48B, Sankaritola Street,
CALCUTTA-14.
The 2nd Dec' 1963.

Secretary

Fig: THE BENGAL MEDICAL UNION, 48B Sankaritola Street, Calcutta-14. Membership Certificate No. BAS-3822, Dated 2nd Dec' 1963 of Dr. Rosman Ali Choudhury.

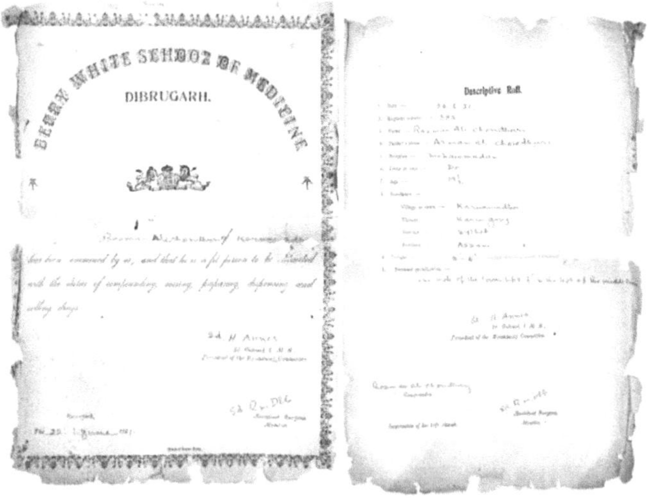

BERRY WHITE SCHOOL OF MEDICINE
DIBRUGARH.

Descriptive Roll.

Fig: Certificate of Dr. Rosman Ali Choudhury from Berry White School of Medicine, Dibrugarh on 22nd June 1921.

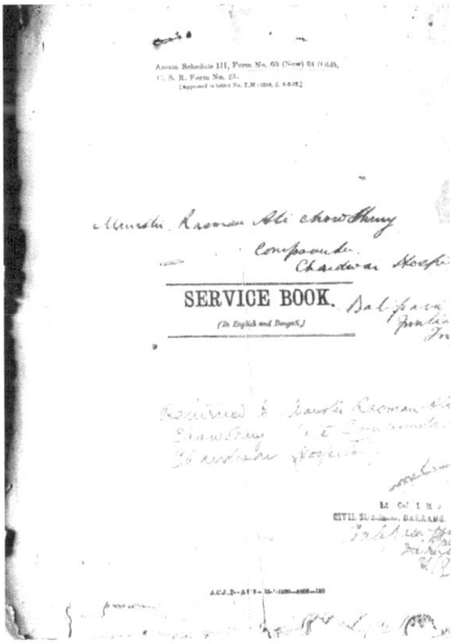

Fig: Sevice Book of
Dr. Rosman Ali Choudhury.

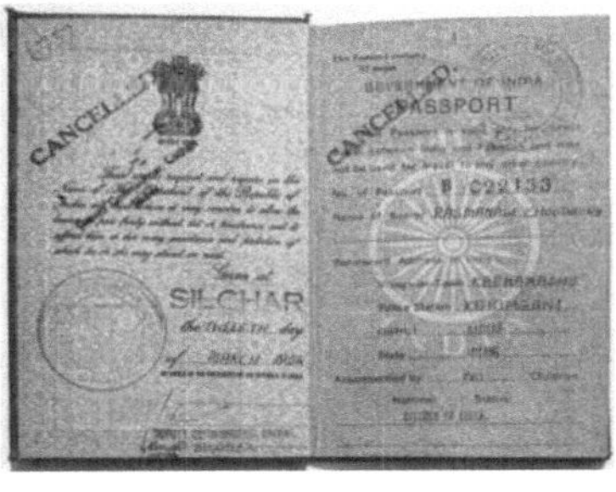

Fig: Passport of Dr. Rosman Ali Choudhury, Dated 12th March 1954 & later renewed on 16th July 1959.

Fig: Passport of Akhtarun Nessa Choudhury
W/o Dr.Rosman Ali Choudhury, Dated 20th December 1957.

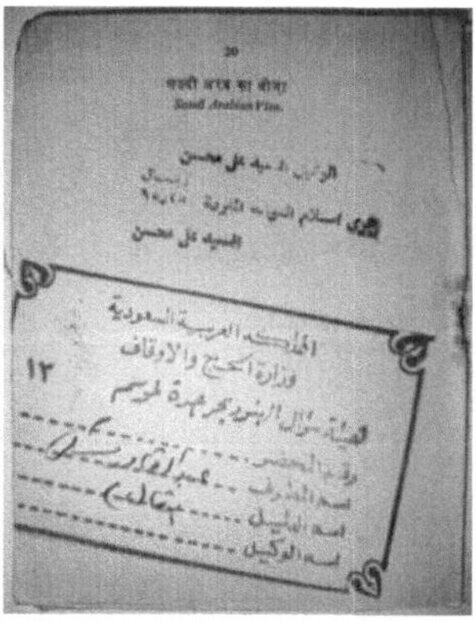

Fig: Pilgrim Pass For Pilgrims Proceeding To The Hejiz From Ports In The States Of India of Dr. Rosman Ali Choudhury, Dated 2nd Jan' 1971.
Port of Embarkation: Bombay.

Fig: Saudi Arabian Visa

The Man Who Named Karimganj

In the quiet banks of the Kushiyara River, where the land breathes the soul of Sylhet, a saint once walked, his name, Shah Abdul Karim (R:). He arrived in Sylhet around 1303 CE accompanying the great Hazrat Shah Jalal Mujarrad-e-Yemeni (R:), as part of the historic spiritual mission to Sylhet. Among the 360 auliyas who came to spread the light of Islam, Shah Abdul Karim held a unique place not only in spiritual lineage but in shaping the very identity of a region.

In 1308 CE, after arriving through the river route, he chose to settle by the banks of the Kushiyara in the area now known as Roynagar, directly facing the present-day Hadargram Jam-e-Masjid. There, he lived a life of piety, teaching the values of Deen (Islamic faith) through humility, simplicity, and profound character. The people of the region, moved by his spiritual conduct and gentle wisdom, began embracing Islam under his guidance.

Around his humble abode, a small marketplace began to flourish. Locals fondly referred to it as Karim Shah'r Bazar the market of Shah Karim. Over time, this name echoed so deeply in the lives of the people that the entire area came to be known as Karimganj, literally meaning "the place or settlement of Karim." Thus, the very name Karimganj stands as a living tribute to this saint whose presence transformed hearts and land alike.

Shah Abdul Karim spent his life serving the people and remained rooted to the soil where he preached. After his passing, he was buried near the Hadargram mosque, where his mazar still stands in solemn remembrance a spiritual anchor in the heart of the valley.

A Soul Not Bound by District Lines

Sylheti continues to thrive not only within Barak Valley but across the world. From London's Brick Lane to Toronto's neighborhoods, from Dubai's tea shops to Kuala Lumpur's Sylheti communities, the language follows its people. Sylheti is now a global language, carried by its diaspora with pride. There are Sylheti radio stations, cultural organisations, podcasts, and even YouTube channels promoting the language internationally. And yet, back home in Barak, it holds deeper meaning. It is a symbol of unity among the three districts, a common thread binding families, communities, and faiths. It is our mother tongue, our collective identity, and a proud torchbearer of our cultural resilience.

Sylheti Music — Our Living Language in Melody

Sylheti music, both traditional and contemporary, continues to resonate across generations. From timeless classics like "Haire Mon Mojare Re," "Dol Dol Doloni," "Bondhu Amar Roila Re," "O Shader Lau", "Aji Bidai Dile," "Bhatir Pola" to recent viral hits like "O Tunir Maa," "Oporadhi," and "Shundori Maiyya E Amar Mon Nilo Kariya," these songs echo in weddings, long drives, village fairs, and even diaspora lounges in London, New York, and Dubai. They serve as emotional anchors, reminders of where we come from, and what we carry within us.

Sylheti Cuisine, Flavour of the Fields and Rivers

The Sylheti kitchen is a world where tradition simmers in every pot, and the essence of the land and rivers finds its way into each bite. Deeply rooted in agrarian and fishing culture, Sylheti cuisine celebrates bold, rustic flavours born from necessity and nurtured by generations. Dishes like shutki maas (fermented or dried fish) carry intense aromas and a depth of taste that may surprise outsiders but feel like comfort to locals. Pabda or baila fish curry, simmered in mustard oil with green chillies, and the delicately pungent kharisa shutki are hallmarks of a cuisine that isn't afraid to make a statement. Rice remains the centerpiece, often served with lentils, leafy vegetables, mashed potatoes (aloo bharta), and pickles that awaken the senses.

Food is rarely just food in Sylheti households, it's emotion. Meals are traditionally enjoyed sitting cross-legged on mats, eaten by hand, where each handful carries warmth, memory, and connection. The act of cooking is often communal, passed from mother to daughter, grandmother to grandchild, forming an oral history flavoured with turmeric and time. Even among Sylheti communities abroad, dishes like ilish bhuna, chunga pitha (bamboo rice cakes) continue to grace the table on special days, preserving identity across continents. For the Sylheti people, cooking is not just sustenance, it is storytelling through spice, patience, and pride.

Traditional Attire – Elegance in Identity

Sylheti traditional attire is more than just fabric, it is a living expression of culture, pride, and continuity. On festive occasions, Sylheti women drape themselves in resplendent silk sarees adorned with shimmering gold borders, often in hues of deep red, royal blue, or emerald green. These sarees, especially the bridal Benarasi, are intricately woven and paired with heirloom jewelry, reflecting both grace and generational wealth. Men complement this elegance by donning crisp kurta-pajamas, often in white or cream, with fine embroidery or a light stole that adds a distinctly Eastern flair. In colder months or ceremonial events, hand-embroidered shawls and turbans further enhance the grandeur. A subtle tilak or a stroke of surma on the eyes is not just aesthetic, it is symbolic of devotion, dignity, and a connection to ancestral traditions. Even among the diaspora in distant cities like London, Dubai, or New York, Sylhetis proudly wear their traditional attire during Eid, weddings, Pohela Boishakh (New Year), and cultural gatherings, reaffirming that identity may travel, but It never fades.

Sylheti Theatre and Comedy — Language With Laughter

Sylheti theatre and skit culture has come a long way, evolving beautifully from humble village stages under banyan trees to widely-viewed YouTube channels followed across continents. What was once performed in open fields during fairs and local gatherings has now found a new digital home, yet its essence remains rooted in the everyday life of the people. This transformation has allowed the art to grow, adapt, and reach new generations without losing the warmth and wit that define Sylheti humour.

Today, channels like বুন্দিয়ার LADDU @bundiyar_ladduuu, Barak Kantha, Northeast Comedians, Kasabangla, Green Bangla, Tipu Khan Entertainment, and ERN Comedy are leading the charge in preserving not just the laughter but also the rich musicality and rhythm of the Sylheti accent. Their content resonates with a wide audience because it reflects real conversations, familiar frustrations, and shared joys. Through sketches, parodies, and playful satire, they capture everything from domestic quirks and social habits to political ironies and village drama. Whether it's the stubborn elder, the over-dramatic aunt, the gossiping neighbour, or the know-it-all youth, these figures feel like they live right next door. The magic lies in how they make people laugh not by mocking others, but by inviting them in to laugh together, as a community.

More than just entertainment, this evolving Sylheti skit culture has become an act of cultural preservation. It safeguards a linguistic identity, revives traditional storytelling, and creates a strong sense of belonging among Sylhetis across the globe. In an age where many regional voices are being drowned out, Sylheti content creators continue to remind us that humour, when drawn from lived experience, becomes both a mirror and a bridge - reflecting who we are and connecting us to where we come from. Let this chapter stand as a declaration: we are Sylheti, not by adoption, but by birth and by belonging.

VII
Forgotten in Policy – The Political Margins of Barak

"যে মাটি অবহেলিত, সেই মাটি একদিন বিস্ময় জাগাবে।"
(রবীন্দ্রনাথ ঠাকুরের দ্বারা অনুপ্রাণিত)
"The soil that is ignored today shall one day awaken wonder."
(Inspired by Rabindranath Tagore)

The Policy Blind Spot

For decades, Barak Valley has been treated as a political afterthought, rarely central to Assam's governance and frequently absent in development schemes, budget allocations, and long-term vision documents.

Despite being home to over 40 lakh people and having three major districts — Cachar, Karimganj, and Hailakandi, the valley remains underfunded, underrepresented, and underestimated. Roads remain broken, hospitals remain few, educational institutions lack infrastructure & industries? Mostly shut down. It is as though Barak exists only during elections, and vanishes from the map when it's time for action.

Dispur and Delhi – A Distant Dream

Barak's problems are not just geographical, they are systemic. Both Dispur (Assam's capital) and Delhi (the national capital) have treated the region with a certain detachment.

- State policies often focus heavily on Upper Assam.
- Flood and disaster relief is delayed or inadequate.
- Cultural promotion, tourism, and industrialization ignore the valley.
- Rail and air connectivity are minimal and unreliable.

Every monsoon, landslides in the Dima Hasao region frequently sever the only rail line connecting Barak to the rest of Assam. Goods are stalled, people are stranded, and essential transport collapses. Sometimes, even emergency medical patients and oxygen tankers are stuck for days. Students miss exams. Daily commuters suffer. Business transactions halt.

With railways cut off, people are forced to rely on high-cost flights, often paying inflated fares due to limited airline services and no government subsidy or price cap (One way flight fare was almost ₹59,000+ from Silchar-Guwahati, during the floods in the year 2022). The average Barak resident pays more for a flight from Silchar to Guwahati than many others pay to fly across states or even internationally. This is not just an inconvenience; it's a form of economic discrimination.

To make matters worse, there is no direct flight from Silchar to major cities like Delhi or Bengaluru, even though thousands of students, professionals, and patients need to travel to these cities regularly. Every trip involves a layover, delay, or rebooking, increasing travel time, costs, and stress.

For patients requiring urgent medical treatment in Delhi AIIMS or Bengaluru's private hospitals, the delay in travel can mean the difference between life and death. For students going to write competitive exams, a cancelled flight could cost a future. For small business owners, it means a lost deal.

Silchar Airport, despite being one of the busiest in the Northeast after Guwahati, still suffers from poor infrastructure, inadequate lounge facilities, frequent flight delays, and zero night landing capabilities. No major investments are being made to modernize it, a reflection of the neglect Barak has come to expect.

People of the Barak Valley often prefer using Agartala's Maharaja Bir Bikram Airport over Silchar Airport because of its better connectivity and affordability. Agartala Airport offers a greater number of flights at comparatively lower fares, along with direct connections to major cities like Kolkata, Guwahati, Delhi, Bengaluru, Chennai, and Mumbai. This makes travel more convenient and cost-effective, especially for those seeking seamless access to important urban centers for education, healthcare, and business purposes.

In contrast, even smaller regions in Upper Assam have received new airport terminals, air routes under the UDAN scheme, and political visits advocating better connectivity.

The Roads That Lead Nowhere

No conversation about Barak's policy neglect is complete without addressing the horrendous road conditions. Roads in Barak Valley are not just bad, they are often life threatening. Major highways, including NH-37, NH-54, and NH-306, which connect Barak Valley to other parts of Assam and Mizoram, are riddled with potholes, sudden craters, collapsed culverts, and washed-out bridges.

During monsoon, these roads turn into mudslides and swamps, causing trucks to overturn, ambulances to stall, and cars to get stuck for hours. Even in dry seasons, daily commuters endure bone-jarring rides, risking their lives and vehicles.

Entire stretches between Silchar and Haflong, or Silchar and Karimganj, remain in a state of perpetual construction or abandonment. Road signage is missing. Lighting is absent. And when accidents occur, which they often do, there's no trauma care center or helpline ready to respond.

In remote villages of Karimganj or Hailakandi, people still walk miles to reach basic health services or ration shops because there is no proper motorable road. School buses can't reach. Doctors hesitate to visit.

In the remote areas of Patharkandi or Badarpur, vehicles break down due to the sheer number of crater-like potholes. Even public buses avoid certain routes, leaving the elderly and poor to walk for kilometers. Every election promises new roads, yet year after year, what Barak gets is a fresh layer of gravel that disappears with the first rains.

Despite repeated appeals and submissions of development proposals, Barak receives only a fraction of the funds allotted for road infrastructure in Assam. Corruption, bureaucratic delays, and regional apathy have ensured that a region that fuels the state with manpower and votes remains physically cut off.

This inaccessibility also hampers tourism, a sector with huge potential in Barak. With natural beauty, historical landmarks, and unique culture, Barak could easily attract visitors, if only one could reach it without fearing for their life on the roads.

Representation without Power

Barak has MPs and MLAs, yes but how much influence do they really hold?

While the Barak Valley is presently represented in the council of ministers, the expectations of the people remain largely unmet. Despite having voices within the ruling establishment, key regional concerns continue to linger without adequate attention. Critical sectors like education, transport, and industry, which are vital to Barak's progress, often find themselves lower on the government's priority list. The presence of ministers has yet to translate into tangible benefits for the valley, raising quiet questions about the effectiveness of representation without active advocacy.

The valley is reduced to a voting ground, not a voice. People often joke bitterly, "Barak votes for governments, but gets forgotten the next morning."

Voices That Don't Echo in Policy

Despite its deep Bengali roots, Barak Valley faces linguistic insecurity, especially in the face of attempts to enforce Assamese-centric cultural policies.

From textbooks to administration, Barak's preferences are often sidelined, Sylheti isn't recognized officially, local dialects and cultural practices aren't preserved, job quotas and exams often overlook Barak's realities.

Why This Matters

Barak Valley is more than just a "region" on the map. It is a living idea, an enduring testament to coexistence, contribution, and identity. It is a land where diverse communities have stood together through history, building bonds that have outlasted political borders and administrative divisions. But even the strongest ideas can begin to erode when they are denied the nourishment of attention and policy support. Neglect does not simply stall development; it slowly chips away at the very spirit of a people who have always believed in giving more than they take.

Policy, therefore, cannot and must not be dictated by population size or the arithmetic of vote bank politics alone. If governance is to be just, it must be guided by need, by decades of neglect, and by the principle of equity. What Barak Valley seeks is not privilege, nor does it demand a special pedestal. It seeks parity, an equal place at the table. It does not wish for extraordinary favours but for the basic recognition that its people deserve the same opportunities, the same infrastructure, and the same dignity as any other part of the nation.

Until that happens, every broken road in the Valley, every cancelled train that cuts off its connectivity, every overpriced flight ticket that keeps its people isolated, and every unemployed graduate who dreams of leaving will stand as a quiet but piercing reminder: this land gave everything-its resources, its resilience, its culture-and in return, it has too often been met with silence. The Barak Valley is not asking for charity. It is asking for justice. And that makes all the difference.

VIII
Barak Valley – A Land of Heritage, Harmony, and Hidden Potential

"The beauty of Barak does not shout — it whispers through its halls of learning and corridors of progress, quietly shaping destinies far beyond its valley."

Notable Establishments – Legacy Institutions of Barak

Barak Valley is home to some of the region's most respected educational, healthcare, and cultural institutions.

The Silchar Railway Station is one of the most important terminals in Northeast India. It connects Barak Valley to other parts of Assam and neighboring states.

Prominent media houses such as Dainik Jugasankha, Nababarta Prasanga play an important role in voicing local concerns and preserving cultural identity. Cultural organizations like Barak Upatyaka Banga Sahitya O Sanskriti Sammelan promote Bengali and Sylheti literature, language, and performing arts.

In Silchar, institutions like Guru Charan University (Erstwhile G.C. College), Cachar College, Assam Central University and the National Institute of Technology (NIT Silchar) are prestigious centers of academic excellence. Silchar Medical College serves as the primary healthcare institution for southern Assam.

In Karimganj, colleges like Karimganj College, Rabindra Sadan Girls' College, and Ramkrishna Nagar College serve thousands of students across disciplines.

Karimganj Government High School, also known locally as Government Boys' Higher Secondary School, is one of the oldest and most prestigious educational institutions in the Barak Valley region of Assam. Established in 1884, during British colonial rule, the school has stood as a beacon of education and discipline for over a century. Located in the heart of Karimganj town, the school has played a foundational role in shaping the academic and moral values of generations of students. Over the years, it has produced numerous scholars, administrators, teachers, and public servants who have contributed significantly to both regional and national development. The school initially began as a boys-only high school and has since evolved into a Higher Secondary School, offering education from Class VI to Class XII, under the Assam state education board. The campus also serves as a cultural and intellectual hub, often hosting district-level debates, science exhibitions, and academic competitions. Despite the rise of private institutions, Karimganj Government High School continues to be respected for its historical significance, disciplined environment, and dedicated teaching faculty. It is not just a school-it is an institution that has witnessed the socio-political transformations of the region, and still stands tall as a symbol of heritage, pride, and public education.

The Akbarpur Agricultural Research Centre, located in Karimganj district, plays a crucial role in the promotion of agricultural education and research in Barak Valley. Established to support scientific farming practices, crop experimentation, and training for local farmers, the centre has become a valuable institution in addressing the unique agricultural needs of the region. It serves as a hub for agronomy research, soil testing, and plant breeding, particularly suited to the climatic and soil conditions of southern Assam. The centre also conducts outreach programmes, workshops, and demonstrations aimed at empowering rural communities with modern and sustainable farming techniques.

The Maizgram Polytechnic, situated in Karimganj district, is an emerging institution focused on providing technical and vocational education to students of the region. It offers diploma-level courses in various engineering and technology disciplines, preparing a skilled workforce for both local industries and broader employment opportunities. The polytechnic has helped bridge the gap between academic education and practical skill development, especially for students from rural and economically weaker sections. With increasing focus on infrastructure development and industry alignment, Maizgram Polytechnic is steadily contributing to the technical empowerment of youth in Barak Valley.

Barak Valley is also known for its network of schools offering quality education, Kendriya Vidyalayas in Silchar and Karimganj serve central government employees' children and others with CBSE education. Maharishi Vidya Mandirs, located across Silchar and other towns, blend traditional Indian values with modern schooling.Preschools and primary education centers like Kidzee, Akmei Global School, Rowlands Public School, and Babyland form the foundation for early childhood development.

Tarabhusan Pal Junior College (formerly Karimganj Junior College of Science) offers higher secondary education in Science, Commerce, and Arts. Karimganj Law College prepares aspiring advocates and legal scholars. Barak Valley Engineering College, established in 2017, is affiliated with Gauhati University and approved by AICTE, providing technical education to the region's students.

Jam-e-ul Uloom Nizamia Title Madrassa: Founded by Hazrat Allama Nizamuddin Bishkuti (R:), an eminent international Islamic scholar of the Indian subcontinent, this madrassa carries forward the spiritual and intellectual heritage of Bishkut Dargah Sharif.

This institution is renowned for its balanced curriculum, integrating:

- Traditional Islamic sciences: Qur'an, Hadith, Fiqh, Tajweed, Aqidah, Hifz, Sufi philosophy
- Modern education: Arabic, Urdu, general curriculum, computer science, and vocational studies
- Human values: Ethics, Islamic history, and civilization

Jam-e-ul Uloom Nizamia remains a beacon of religious and academic excellence, fostering cross-border spiritual and educational linkages in the Barak–Sylhet region.

Markaz-ul-Uloom Bhanga Sharif Madrassa (Established 1942): Founded by Shaykh-ul-Islam Syed Hussain Ahmed Madani, a renowned nationalist freedom fighter and former President of Jamiat Ulama-e-Hind, this madrassa in Bhanga Sharif, Karimganj stands as a symbol of Islamic education and patriotism.

Affiliated with Darul Uloom Deoband, the madrassa offers courses up to the Aliya level and specializes in: Qur'anic sciences and Hadith, Hifz and Tajweed, Arabic and Islamic jurisprudence (Fiqh). Markaz-ul-Uloom has produced generations of scholars and imams and continues to play a major role in the religious and cultural fabric of the region.

Deorail Senior Madrassa & Deorail Darul Hadis Title Madrassa (Badarpur): These two prominent institutions were established by Abu Yusuf Mohammad Yakub Badarpuri (1854–1958), a revered Sufi scholar, educationist, and freedom fighter from Bundashil, Badarpur. After extensive studies in Cuttack, Calcutta, and Rampur, he returned to devote his life to spiritual and educational reform. Both the Madrassa focuses on: Islamic sciences including Hadith, Qur'anic studies, Fiqh, and Sufism, Community-based education, especially among the marginalized.

Though more about him is covered in the “Eminent Personalities of the Valley” chapter, his educational legacy endures through these institutions and his many disciples worldwide.

Darul Uloom Banskandi Madrassa- an Islamic seminary founded by Sheikh-ul-Hadith Hazrat Maulana Ahmed Ali Saheb, a center for Islamic learning, has long contributed to religious scholarship in the region. With its longstanding history, it draws visitors interested in theology, education, and historical institutions.

Madinatul Uloom Bagbari (المدرسة العالية النجيبية مدينة العلوم بباغباري), established on 1st February 1873 by Najib Ali Choudhury, formerly known as Madinatul Uloom Bagbari Najibia Alia Madrasa, is a historic Islamic seminary located in Bagbari, Karimganj district, in the Indian state of Assam. It is widely regarded as the oldest Islamic educational institution in South Assam. The madrasa was founded in 1873 by Najib Ali Choudhury, an eminent Islamic scholar of the region. According to oral tradition, while residing in Mecca, Najib Ali Choudhury had a dream in which the Prophet Muhammad ﷺ instructed him to return to his homeland and dedicate himself to spreading Islamic education. In response, he established the madrasa in his own home in the village of Bagbari. The institution was officially named in Choudhury's honour, and functioned from its original location for nearly a century before shifting to its present campus in 1969. Modelled after Darul Uloom Deoband, which had been established a few years earlier, the madrassa became the first formal Islamic seminary in the region, providing a structured curriculum in place of earlier informal religious teaching.

Initially, it offered instruction up to the level of "Sharh-e-Jami", and later expanded to include the advanced "Dawra-e-Hadith" course after 1992. Over its 150-year history, Madinatul Uloom Bagbari has played a pivotal role in producing Islamic scholars, particularly in the Greater Sylhet region. It remains a respected center for Arabic language and Islamic studies in northeast India.

The Ujandihi Jamiululum Mohammodiya Madrassa, established by Syed Khaled Ahmed Madani at Ujandihi Mezo Saheb Bari, was founded with the aim of spreading both Islamic and modern education. The quality of teaching at this madrassa is widely regarded as exceptional. The institution also houses an orphanage where orphan students reside in the hostel. All necessities, including books, clothing, food, and lodging, are provided free of cost. The expenses are managed through contributions from the local community and donations from disciples. The Madrassa is affiliated with the CMIS Board.

Syed Khaled Ahmed Madani, the founder, is the second son of Shah Sufi Syed Rafiqul Islam Madani Al-Hussaini (R.A.), an eminent Islamic scholar of North East India. He also serves as an Executive Member of the Human Rights International Federation.

In conclusion, the Barak Valley has long been home to a constellation of esteemed institutions that have played a pivotal role in shaping the region's intellectual, cultural, and spiritual landscape for countless generations. These institutions—whether they were centers of learning, places of worship, cultural hubs, or forums of public discourse—have been the very lifeblood of the valley's identity. They nurtured young minds with education and discipline, instilled timeless values of compassion, unity, and service, and stood as enduring pillars of resilience through times of change, uncertainty, and adversity.

Over the decades, these institutions have produced an extraordinary lineage of men and women who have excelled in diverse fields such as law, politics, literature, education, social reform, and public service. Many among them rose to prominence at both state and national levels, bringing honour and recognition not only to the Barak Valley but to the entire nation. Others went on to contribute globally, earning distinction in international forums and advancing causes that transcended geographical boundaries. Equally remarkable were those who chose to remain closer to home, devoting their lives to uplifting their local communities, preserving the valley's unique cultural heritage, and ensuring that its traditions of tolerance and harmony endured for future generations.

The Barak Valley has also given rise to revered figures in Sufism and religious teachings whose wisdom, moral strength, and spiritual guidance shaped the lives of countless people. Their influence extended far beyond the valley's borders, inspiring communities across India and even in distant lands. Through their words and actions, they championed a vision of humanity rooted in faith, ethical living, and the collective pursuit of justice and peace.

The contributions of these individuals and institutions have left a lasting imprint on society, enriching the valley's progressive outlook while strengthening its spiritual foundation. They have demonstrated how intellectual pursuit and moral conviction can coexist to create a society that thrives both materially and spiritually. Moreover, their work has not only uplifted the Barak Valley but has also played a vital role in shaping the cultural and moral fabric of the country at large, with ripples felt far beyond national boundaries.

In Chapter 23, we will look more closely at the lives, struggles, and achievements of these remarkable individuals. Their stories will serve as an inspiration not only for the people of the Barak Valley but for generations everywhere, proving that a small region can illuminate the world through its ideas, its resilience, and its commitment to higher ideals.

IX
Heritage Trails — The Tourism and Historic Legacy of Barak Valley

Unearth the unseen. Experience Barak.

Barak Valley, often overlooked in the broader tourism circuits of Northeast India, is a region rich in natural splendor, spiritual harmony, and cultural history. Its rivers, hills, spiritual shrines, and heritage spots reflect a deep connection between people and place between past and present.

Malegarh – War Memorial Add Sepoy Mutiny
The Malegarh War Memorial, located near the village of Latu in the Karimganj district of Assam, stands as a poignant reminder of a lesser-known but deeply significant episode of the Indian freedom struggle. It commemorates the battle fought on 18 December 1857 during the First War of Indian Independence, popularly known as the Sepoy Mutiny. A group of Indian rebel sepoys from the 34th Native Infantry, based in Chittagong (now in Bangladesh), were on their way to join forces in Manipur. As they moved through the Sylhet and Karimganj regions, they were intercepted by British troops under the command of Major Byng of the Sylhet Light Infantry.

A fierce battle took place at a small hillock locally known as Rontilla, now referred to as Malegarh. In this confrontation, 26 Indian sepoys and 5 British soldiers, including Major Byng, lost their lives. The Indian sepoys were buried on the very hill where they fell, and over time, the site came to be revered by locals who considered it hallowed ground. These graves, along with relics from the battle-such as pistols, swords, and cannons-have been preserved, symbolizing the region's silent but proud participation in the national uprising of 1857.

The Malegarh War Memorial was later constructed atop the hill to honor these fallen heroes. Each year on 18 December, the site comes alive with commemorative events organized by local administration, the Border Security Force (BSF), NGOs like the Patkai Trekker group, and citizens from across the Barak Valley. Ceremonies include floral tributes, lighting of lamps to honor each martyr, and cultural performances. These rituals not only pay homage but also educate the younger generation about the courage and sacrifices made by these freedom fighters.

Despite its historical importance, the site has long suffered from neglect and underdevelopment. Activists, historians, and residents have called for the Assam government to recognize Malegarh as a protected heritage site. Proposals have included improved road access, installation of lights, construction of visitor facilities, and even the establishment of a museum and auditorium to promote historical tourism. There have also been appeals to include the story of Malegarh in the school curriculum to ensure that future generations understand its importance.

Malegarh represents more than just a battle; it embodies a moment where local soil bore witness to the earliest flames of India's freedom movement. As the nation strives to preserve its historical memory, Malegarh stands as a powerful symbol of forgotten valor, unity, and resistance-a sacred ground that deserves national recognition and enduring reverence.

Martyrs' Tomb & Gandhi Bagh Shahid Smarak, Silchar
The Martyrs' Tomb and Shahid Smarak at Gandhi Bagh, located in the heart of Silchar, is one of the most emotionally powerful landmarks in Barak Valley. It commemorates the language martyrs of the 1961 Bengali Language Movement, during which eleven brave individuals were killed in police firing while protesting for the recognition of Bengali as an official language in the Barak region of Assam. Their sacrifice marked a turning point in Assam's linguistic and cultural politics.

Today, the memorial stands as a solemn symbol of resistance, cultural pride, and democratic protest. Every year on May 19, thousands gather here to observe Bhasha Shahid Divas, paying tribute to the martyrs and reaffirming their commitment to preserving their linguistic heritage. Gandhi Bagh, with its well-maintained garden and memorial structures, serves not only as a site of remembrance but also as a civic space for reflection, pride, and historical consciousness in the valley.

Mughal Historical Fort of Badarpur
The Mughal Historical Fort of Badarpur, located in Karimganj district, is a significant yet lesser-known remnant of Mughal military architecture in Assam.

Strategically situated along the banks of the Barak River, this fort once served as a frontline outpost of the Mughal Empire during their expansion into the eastern frontier. It was likely administered by Mughal Faujdars (military governors) who oversaw defense, trade, and tax collection in the region. The fort's location was of immense importance, as Badarpur functioned as a gateway to the Barak Valley, connecting Bengal with the hill kingdoms and inner Assam. Though now in ruins, traces of earthen ramparts, moats, and structural foundations still survive, providing insight into the strategic planning of Mughal-era fortifications. Local legends and scattered historical records suggest it witnessed multiple military movements, including skirmishes with hill tribes and later resistance against colonial expansion. Despite its historical value, the site remains largely unprotected and undocumented, awaiting proper archaeological attention and conservation. Reviving and preserving this fort could contribute significantly to the heritage tourism circuit of Barak Valley, highlighting the region's role in the broader canvas of Mughal and subcontinental history.

Kachari Fort of Khaspur

In contrast, the Kachari Fort of Khaspur, situated about 20 kilometers west of Silchar in Cachar district, is more architecturally expressive and culturally significant. It was the capital of the Dimasa Kachari Kingdom, a powerful indigenous dynasty that once ruled large parts of Assam, including the Barak Valley. The ruins at Khaspur include remnants of royal palaces, ceremonial gates, temples, and administrative buildings that showcase the traditional Dimasa architectural style. Among its most iconic features is the elephant gate, symbolizing royal authority and grandeur. The layout of the site suggests a well-planned capital with both spiritual and military functions. The Dimasa kings ruled from this location until their kingdom merged with British-administered Assam in the 19th century. Even in its ruined state, Khaspur stands as a proud reminder of indigenous rule and cultural identity in Assam's historical narrative. It is a popular destination for students, researchers, and tourists, especially during festivals and cultural events.

Together, these two forts, Badarpur and Khaspur, tell the story of Barak Valley's dual legacy of Mughal influence and native dynastic power. They are essential landmarks that reflect the valley's strategic importance, political transitions, and rich cultural layers across centuries. With thoughtful conservation, tourism planning, and historical interpretation, these sites can be revitalized as educational and cultural heritage destinations for future generations.

Natural Beauty and Scenic Spots:

The landscape of Barak Valley is defined by the serene flows of the **Barak**, **Kushiyara**, and **Longai rivers**. The picturesque hills around **Ratabari**, adorned with lush rubber gardens, provide visitors with a refreshing experience, ideal for eco-tourism.

One of the most notable natural attractions is **Son Beel,** located in Karimganj district of Assam, is one of the largest seasonal wetlands in Asia and a unique natural treasure of Barak Valley. Spanning thousands of hectares, the beel (or lake) transforms dramatically with the seasons-serving as a vast flooded lake during the monsoon and turning into rich agricultural land in the dry season. This dual nature not only supports fishing and farming livelihoods but also enhances its ecological significance. Son Beel is home to a variety of migratory birds, freshwater fish, and aquatic flora, making it a paradise for birdwatchers, ecologists, and photographers. Its breathtaking sunsets and endless water horizons give it a near-mystical charm. While still underexplored, Son Beel has immense potential for sustainable tourism and wetland conservation, if supported by proper infrastructure and community engagement.

Sindhura, another scenic area, offers panoramic views and peaceful retreats for those looking to escape urban chaos, a serene destination known for its breathtaking viewpoints, natural tranquility, and village charm. Often overlooked by commercial tourists, Sindhura offers an authentic slice of rural Barak, with its mist-covered mornings, green slopes, and a peaceful atmosphere that soothes the spirit. It's a favorite among locals for picnics, short treks, and quiet retreats.

Another captivating destination in Barak Valley is **Dolu Lake**, located approximately 11 kilometers from Silchar. Nestled amidst gentle hills and lush greenery, the lake offers a peaceful retreat for nature lovers and casual travelers alike. Its calm waters and serene surroundings make it an ideal spot for picnics, boating, and birdwatching. Over the years, it has grown in popularity as a local getaway, especially during weekends and holidays. Despite its natural beauty, the lake remains relatively underdeveloped in terms of tourism infrastructure, making it a hidden gem with vast potential. With proper conservation and eco-tourism initiatives, Dolu Lake could emerge as one of the leading natural attractions in southern Assam.

Malidor, situated near Digorkhal in Cachar district, is a scenic spot along the Assam-Meghalaya border that offers a blend of natural beauty and cultural significance. The Malidor River flows quietly through this area, acting as a natural boundary between the two states. Surrounded by gentle hills, dense greenery, and rural settlements, Malidor provides a peaceful setting for visitors seeking an escape into nature. The location is notable not only for its geography but also for the intercultural coexistence between communities of Assam and Meghalaya. Though still off the radar of mainstream tourism, Malidor holds great promise for eco-tourism, borderland exploration, and quiet countryside retreats.

Narayan Dhar, The River Island of Lakhipur, nestled in the serene waters of the Barak River, Narayan Dhar is a picturesque river island located in Lakhipur subdivision of Cachar district. This natural island holds both religious and ecological significance. It is home to a revered temple of Lord Vishnu, making it a popular pilgrimage site for local devotees and visitors from nearby areas.

The island is situated within the wider Barak Valley, a region characterized by its rivers, plains, and hills. The Barak River, which originates in Manipur and flows through Mizoram and Assam before entering Bangladesh, stretches over 900 kilometers. It plays a central role in shaping the geography and ecosystem of the valley.

Narayan Dhar lies along the navigable stretch of the Barak River, from Lakhipur to Bhanga (121 kilometers), a section officially declared as National Waterway 6 in 2016. The river and its tributaries – Jiri, Jatinga, Sonai, and Daleswari, contribute to the rich biodiversity of the region, supporting a variety of flora and fauna. The tranquil setting of Narayan Dhar, combined with its spiritual ambiance, makes it an emerging destination for riverine tourism and nature retreats.

Gua Bari, located near Banskandi in Cachar district, is a place of historical and cultural interest in Barak Valley. The name "Gua Bari" roughly translates to "Betel Nut House," and it is often associated with ancient trade routes and settlement patterns of the region. The site is locally known for its natural beauty, surrounded by serene greenery and traditional rural landscapes. Gua Bari also holds significance for those interested in tracing the folklore, myths, and oral histories of Barak Valley's past.
Though not yet developed as a mainstream tourist destination, its rustic charm and cultural associations make it a place worth exploring for those seeking offbeat heritage experiences.

Spiritual Harmony and Sacred Sites:
Barak Valley is a cradle of interfaith harmony. In Karimganj, the **Bishkut Dargah Sharif** is a sacred, traditional, historical and well-known religious land of this Indian sub-continent. Silsila A Bishkuti has millions of followers scattered around the world. Although they live in different parts of the world, but this holy land always attracts their spiritual mind and they love and respect this holy land from their soul. So they have a close soul connection with this holy land.

In the year 2018, the Government of Assam recognised Bishkut Dargah Sharif as a spiritual, historical shrine and started it's progress under Assam Darshan Scheme for the preservation and development, which is one of the most sacred holy lands of this sub-continent.

On 22nd Falgoon of every Bengali year, here in its premises held Ajimusshan Mehfil-e-Twarikot, thousands of people of all castes, creed, community, race and religion of the neighbouring states attend this holy mehfil. The mehfil ends after the akheri monajat; prays dua to the Almighty for universal peace and prosperity, life and lives before and after death. Besides that a tasty tabarruq; shirni is distributed to all. 'Bishkut Dargah Sharif Preservation And Development Trust' is a cheritable institution working for the preservation and development of Bishkut Dargah Sharif and its various establishments i.e., Dargah Jam-e-Masjid, Bishkut Dargah Sharif Madrassa, Mazar Sharif, Khanqah[6], Musafirkhana[7], Langarkhana[8] etc. Advocate Abdul Muqtadir Choudhury, Ex Minister Assam is the Managing Trustee and Educator Mamazzad Ahmed Choudhury (Babu) is the Executive Trustee of the

[6] A spiritual retreat or lodge where Sufi live, teach and guide disciples.
[7] Guest House
[8] Community kitchen

Trustee Committee. On the 14 of Jaista of Bengali year, celebrates the Death Anniversary of Shah Sufi Hazrat Maulana Mohammed Mashood Bishkuti (R:) and on the 23rd March celebrates the death anniversary of Shah Sufi Hazrat Allama Nizam Uddin Bishkuti (R:) Bishkut Dargah Sharif Preservation and Development Trust, requests everyone's presence and cooperation.

Bhuvan Pahar, located in the Cachar district of Assam, stands as one of the most revered and spiritually significant sites in the Barak Valley. Rising amidst the lush greenery and rolling terrain, this hill is not only a natural landmark but also a center of deep religious and cultural importance for the Hindu community, especially for the devotees of Lord Shiva. The hill derives its name from the legendary Bhubaneshwar Mahadev, a form of Lord Shiva believed to reside atop the hill. The sacred Bhuban temple, nestled at the summit, draws thousands of pilgrims every year, particularly during the auspicious festival of Shivaratri, when devotees undertake a challenging trek to offer prayers. The journey is not merely physical but spiritual, symbolizing devotion, endurance, and faith. Apart from its religious significance, Bhuban Pahar is also valued for its breathtaking natural beauty. Dense forests, rare flora and fauna, and panoramic views of the surrounding valley make it a destination for nature lovers and trekkers alike. The serene environment and the rhythmic chanting of pilgrims create an atmosphere that feels timeless and divine. Bhuvan Hill has also become a symbol of unity in the region. People from various backgrounds and communities participate in the pilgrimage, reinforcing a sense of shared heritage and collective faith. The hill's prominence in folklore, oral traditions, and local beliefs further enriches its cultural value. In essence, Bhuvan Pahar is not just a geographical feature - it is a living monument of faith, tradition, and nature's grandeur, echoing the spiritual heartbeat of the Barak Valley.

St. Thomas Church, Silchar, established during the colonial era in Tarapur, is one of the oldest Protestant churches in the region. Built with red bricks in the British architectural style, it continues to serve the Church of North India (CNI) community. Another notable landmark is the Our Lady of the Holy Rosary Catholic Church in Ambicapatty, Silchar. It is a central point of worship and community outreach for Roman Catholics.

Additionally, there are various **Baptist, Evangelical, and Presbyterian churches** spread across Hailakandi and Karimganj, especially in areas with tribal Christian populations. These institutions often double as schools and missionary centers, continuing the legacy of early Christian missionaries in Northeast India. Though Christianity is a minority faith in the Barak Valley, the region is home to several historically and culturally significant churches, particularly in urban centers like Silchar and Karimganj. These churches serve as spiritual, educational, and community hubs for both Bengali and tribal Christian populations.

Gurudwara Sri Guru Singh Sabha stands as a symbol of faith and service in the heart of Silchar town. Though Sikhism is not widely practiced in the Barak Valley, this Gurudwara has become a spiritual and cultural hub for the region's small but active Sikh community, which includes business owners, defense personnel, and long-settled families. The Gurudwara is known for its langar, regular prayers, and social service activities, embodying the core Sikh principles of seva (selfless service) and sarbat da bhala[9]. It welcomes visitors of all faiths, serving as an Inclusive and peaceful space in the multicultural fabric of Barak Valley.

In Badarpur, the resting place and shrine of **Shah Sufi Hazrat Adam Khaki (R:),** was a close companion of Hazrat Shah Jalal Mujarrad-e-Yemeni (R:). He arrived in the Barak Valley after the Conquest of Sylhet in 1303, dedicating his life to the spread of Islam, spiritual enlightenment, and social reform. Settling in Badarpur in present-day Karimganj district in the year 1306 CE. He became a beacon of guidance for local communities. His khanqah evolved into a center of learning and spiritual wisdom, drawing both Hindus and Muslims, and serving as a symbol of harmony and humanism. Today, his shrine in Badarpur remains a revered dargah, visited by countless devotees who come to seek blessings and inspiration from his legacy. Adam Khaki's life and teachings continue to embody the ideals of compassion, unity, and service to humanity, leaving a lasting imprint on the cultural and spiritual fabric of the Barak Valley..

The religious unity of Barak is further seen through landmarks like the **Town Kali Bari Temple**, and the **Church** on Church Road, reflecting a peaceful blend of multiple faiths.

Tea Gardens and Countryside Charm:
The Barak Valley, particularly the Cachar district, has a long and rich history of tea cultivation dating back to 1855, when the British initiated tea plantations in the region. The valley's fertile soil, abundant rainfall, and moderate climate made it ideal for growing high-quality tea. Since then, the

---

[9] welfare of all

industry has flourished, becoming one of the key contributors to the region's economy and cultural identity.

Today, Barak Valley boasts **217 tea gardens**, of which 92 are classified as large estates, while the remaining 125 are small tea gardens. These tea estates not only offer scenic beauty and historical significance but also present opportunities for eco-tourism and tea tourism. Visitors can explore the lush green plantations, observe tea plucking and processing, and engage with the lives of tea garden workers, many of whom belong to the Tea Tribes, a vibrant and culturally distinct community.

The valley's tea culture adds another vibrant layer to its identity. The **Hilara**, **Hatikhira**, **Ayla Bari Tea Estates & others** offer lush, green expanses and a glimpse into Barak's colonial-era economy. These estates are not only economic assets but also visually delightful, attracting photographers, nature lovers, and those interested in the tea production process.

Border Tourism:

Sutarkandi, situated near Karimganj, serves as a vital land **border between India and Bangladesh**. What makes it unique is the presence of a riverine (water) border near Karimganj's Main Post Office. These borders are more than geopolitical features, they symbolize centuries of shared history, trade, and culture. With structured tourism development, Sutarkandi and its surrounding regions can evolve into cross-border heritage hubs.

Historical Townships and Local Legends:

One cannot mention Karimganj without bringing up its iconic **Santar Bazar** — a lively commercial hub teeming with character. Interestingly, the place was officially named Center Bazar, given its central location in the town.

However, the people of Karimganj affectionately turned it into Santar Bazar, a name that stuck over generations. This market has been the beating heart of the town's economy, culture, and street life. With a medley of shops, vendors, eateries, and foot traffic, Santar Bazar encapsulates the hustle and humor of everyday life in Karimganj.

The **old Noti Khal (actually Naughty Canal, named by the British)**, a canal once vital for river trade, and structures like the **Earl Bridge (Now Pulor Upor)** in Karimganj, built during the British era, stand as relics of the colonial past. These areas once thrived with merchants, pilgrims, and travelers, and still echo those footsteps today.

The Barak Valley's beauty lies not in artificial constructs but in the harmony of its past, people, and nature. With sustainable development and increased visibility, it has the potential to emerge as one of the most compelling cultural and eco-tourism destinations in Northeast India.

How to Reach Barak Valley – The Gateway to the South:

Reaching Barak Valley particularly the districts of Silchar, Karimganj, and Hailakandi can often be challenging due to its remote location and weak infrastructure. Yet, the journey into the valley rewards visitors with scenic views, warm hospitality, and unique culture.

By Air:

- Silchar Airport is the only airport in the region, located about 25 km from the city.
- It offers regular flights to Guwahati and Kolkata.

- There are no direct flights to major cities like Delhi or Bengaluru.
- During monsoons or disruptions like landslides, flight tickets become unaffordably expensive due to demand spikes.
- Through Agartala's Maharaja Bir Bikram Airport, which is approximately 226 km by road from Karimganj & 274.5 km from Silchar.

By Train:
Silchar Railway Station is a terminal connected by broad gauge via Lumding to Guwahati.
Major trains include:

- Agartala Rajdhani Express (connects via Badarpur)
- Poorvottar Sampark Kranti Express
- Silchar–Sealdah Kanchanjunga Express

Karimganj and Badarpur Junction provide alternative connectivity, especially for local routes. Landslides and flooding frequently disrupt train schedules, particularly in the Lumding–Haflong hill section.

By Road:

- Silchar is linked by NH-6 and NH-37, but these highways are often in poor condition.
- The Jatinga–Haflong stretch is especially vulnerable to landslides, potholes, and erosion.
- Public and private buses, shared Sumos, Innovas, Ertigas, and taxis run between the valley's towns, but lack of 4-lane roads makes the journey longer than it should be.

Local Transport:

- Local travel within towns is largely dependent on auto-rickshaws, battery rickshaws, and tuk-tuks.
- App-based services like Ola or Uber are rarely available, except in parts of Silchar.

The Barak Valley's transport network-by air, rail, and road remains a critical bottleneck in its journey toward inclusive growth. While Silchar Airport and major railway stations like Silchar and Badarpur provide essential links to other parts of the country, they are often disrupted by natural calamities such as landslides, floods, and seasonal monsoon damage.

Road travel, especially along vulnerable stretches like Jatinga-Haflong, is plagued by poor maintenance, erosion, and narrow highways that extend travel time and reduce safety. The lack of direct flights to major metros, coupled with high airfare during emergencies, further deepens the region's isolation.

These challenges not only limit the ease of movement for residents but also restrict economic investment, tourism, medical access, and timely disaster response.

The heavy reliance on auto-rickshaws and the absence of app-based transport services reflect the urgent need for modernization at the local level. To bridge the gap between potential and progress, the region requires sustained government attention, investment in durable infrastructure, and a focus on climate-resilient transport solutions. Without it, the valley's aspirations will continue to be held back by its physical inaccessibility.

X
Media, Representation, and The Silence Around Barak

"When a region's voice is unheard, its truth is rewritten by others."

The Barak Valley, despite its cultural depth and historical importance, has often found itself missing or misrepresented in the media landscape of Assam and India. While other regions have been given platforms to shape their identity and narrative, Barak's stories have too frequently remained in the shadows.

Invisible on the News Map

From regional news channels to national media outlets, Barak Valley rarely makes headlines unless in moments of tragedy, disaster, or political turmoil. Festivals, literary events, youth innovations, environmental challenges, and cultural milestones are consistently ignored. This erasure creates a skewed image of the region: as backward, disengaged, or insignificant.

Mainstream Assamese media often centers Brahmaputra Valley events, sidelining Barak's linguistic and socio-political uniqueness. In digital media too, most Assamese platforms underrepresent Barak's issues, unless they serve a political narrative.

This absence also discourages students and aspiring journalists from Barak Valley, who grow up without seeing their realities reflected on TV or in print. Many talents remain hidden due to this vacuum, waiting for a story, a camera, a microphone that never arrives.

Digital Rise: Barak's Own Platforms

Although often sidelined by state or national media, Barak Valley has developed its own vibrant media ecosystem. Platforms like Barak Bulletin deliver instant updates and live coverage of local events, helping bridge the gap between mainstream silence and grassroots awareness. Northeast Today (NE Today) frequently features Barak-centric stories, drawing attention to both crises and culture.

Local journalists like Krishna Kanta Sinha from Silchar and Sujan Deb Roy from Karimganj are examples of dedicated reporters who keep the valley's issues alive through independent digital journalism. Platforms like Karimganj Today serve the town with regional updates and voices that would otherwise go unheard.

Despite resource constraints, these digital warriors are reclaiming space, one update, article, or photograph at a time.

Other rising outlets such as Barak Valley Updates, Silchar News, and are also contributing to this decentralised media renaissance. Hyperlocal coverage of civic issues, language rights, student movements, and cultural events has made these pages essential to Barak's new media identity.

Together, these agencies and individuals are proving that Barak's narrative doesn't need outside validation it needs internal amplification.

Beyond Clicks: Journalism as Resistance

In Barak, journalism isn't just a profession, it is resistance. It is an act of defiance against being forgotten. Every blog post, news bulletin, or video documentary becomes a thread in the region's broader tapestry of identity.

These storytellers often face economic and logistical challenges: poor infrastructure, lack of institutional support, and limited reach. Yet, they persist. They record floods when no news van arrives. They livestream protests when no anchor pays attention. They profile achievers when no mainstream platform cares.
A new generation of media enthusiasts, especially students and creatives, are now using platforms like Instagram, Facebook Reels, YouTube, and even podcasts to spotlight Barak's issues. Pages like Voices from Barak, Silchar Lens, and Karimganj Weekly are slowly creating an alternative archive.

The Cost of Silence
Lack of representation doesn't just harm pride, it harms policy. Funding decisions, disaster responses, educational resources, and political appointments are often skewed in favor of more visible regions. When Barak Valley remains on the margins of mainstream discourse, its floods fail to get national attention, its unemployment crisis stays unaddressed, and its infrastructure gaps or health struggles are reduced to local whispers that rarely reach decision-makers.

This isn't just neglect, it is structural injustice. When a region is kept outside the media spotlight, it becomes easier to deny it development, delay justice, and distort its story. The narratives of progress and opportunity often skip over Barak, reinforcing a cycle where underrepresentation leads to underinvestment and vice versa.

Students in Barak grow up rarely seeing role models who speak their dialect, share their cultural identity, or represent their towns in state and national discussions. This lack of positive visibility has long-term effects on aspirations, confidence, and civic engagement. It can erode a young person's belief that their voice matters, reducing the likelihood of them striving for positions of influence. Over time, this invisibility shapes the region's collective psyche, making it harder for communities to demand what they rightfully deserve.

Changing this pattern is not just about pride; it is about ensuring fairness and equal opportunity. Representation determines whose stories are told, whose struggles are acknowledged, and ultimately, whose lives are improved through policy and development.

Reclaiming the Mic

Representation is power. The people of Barak Valley are beginning to understand this truth more deeply than ever before. For far too long, their voices have been overlooked, their contributions sidelined, and their stories left untold. But silence is no longer an option. Barak Valley is learning to speak up through journalism that questions the status quo, through art that carries the weight of lived experiences, through activism that demands justice, and through cultural expressions that celebrate the soul of the region.

What is not given will be built. If resources are denied, communities will come together to create their own. If recognition is withheld, Barak Valley will carve its name into the nation's consciousness. What is not shown will be filmed. The camera will become a weapon of truth, documenting lives and landscapes that deserve to be seen. And what is not heard will be sung. Melodies and lyrics will rise from the valley to echo across the country, telling the world who they are and why they matter.

Let the nation know this clearly. Barak does not wait to be remembered. It refuses to be a footnote in history or a forgotten corner on the map. It rises again and again to be recognized for its resilience, its intellect, its culture, and its people. Every struggle faced and every injustice endured fuels a determination to stand taller, speak louder, and demand the respect it has always deserved.

Let this chapter serve as a reminder, not just for the people of Barak Valley but for anyone who has ever felt invisible. Barak does not need permission to exist. It does not seek approval from those who have ignored it. What it needs is a platform to amplify its voice, respect for its history and contributions, and above all the chance to be heard on its own terms.

XI
Not Sribhumi: It Was, It Is Karimganj

"Names are not labels; they are the lifeblood of memory."

In November 2024, a decision was passed in the Assam state cabinet that struck deep into the hearts of the people of Karimganj, the town, the land, and the name they identified with was to be altered, transformed from its historically rooted name to a new, state sanctioned identity: Sribhumi. This decision, introduced under the Bharatiya Janata Party (BJP) led government in Assam and justified by references to poetic and cultural heritage, sparked not celebration, but a storm of resistance from the people of the region. What followed was not simply a protest over a name but an uprising of memory, a defense of identity, history, and belonging.

Karimganj is not just a name on a map. It is a memory etched in the language of its people, in the curves of the Barak river, in the layered bricks of its old buildings, and in the blood spilled during the 1961 Bengali Language Movement. In a region that has witnessed partition, displacement, and the slow erosion of regional voices, Karimganj stood as a cultural bastion of resilience. The imposition of a new name "Sribhumi" was seen not as a homage to its heritage but as an administrative rewriting of a lived and emotional history.

The official reason cited by the state government for the renaming was poetic, that the land had been described in the works of Rabindranath Tagore as "Sribhumi," a term signifying prosperity, divinity, and cultural wealth. Yet, for most residents, the change did not feel poetic. It felt forced, artificial, and devoid of consultation. The narrative being pushed was one that sanitized and generalized local

identity into something broader, more mythical, and more politically convenient. Karimganj was not simply being renamed; it was being rebranded.
The first response came quietly. A few local poets and journalists wrote critical columns. School teachers discussed the implications in their classrooms. Parents complained to school boards about textbooks preemptively printing the new name. Then came the petitions. Then came the streets.

On the final day of December 2024, the resistance crescendoed. Citizens of Karimganj signed a formal memorandum and staged a mass demonstration. Students from colleges, elders from neighborhoods, cultural activists, religious leaders they all came together in what became one of the largest peaceful gatherings in the recent political history of Barak Valley. Placards rose with sharp, poignant slogans: “Manchi na, manbo na,” means “we have not accepted, we’ll not accept it’.

This was not just about Karimganj alone. Even though protests did not physically occur in Silchar or Hailakandi, the broader emotion simmered across the entire Barak Valley. WhatsApp statuses, local news headlines, Facebook live events, Instagram reels, all reverberated with the emotion of rejection and reaffirmation..

Meanwhile, in press conferences and television debates, government spokespersons defended the change as being rooted in culture and spirituality. They claimed it was apolitical. But the people of Karimganj were not convinced. For them, renaming was not a trivial change. It was political precisely because it attempted to redefine their shared memory without involving them.

The Barak-Sylheti identity is delicate. It is not just Bengali, It Is Barak Bengali, deeply Sylheti, carrying the accent, the songs, the rituals, and the wounds of a past segmented by the 1947 Sylhet referendum. When Sylhet joined East Pakistan, Karimganj remained in India, not by popular will, but by river demarcation. Since then, the people of Karimganj have carried the burden of cultural separation. They lost their direct family connections, their trade networks, their educational centers. In return, they received suspicion, negligence, and now a name that erases their past.

The rejection of the name Sribhumi did not emerge from a vacuum. It emerged from centuries of continuity, shaped by language, migration, religious coexistence, and resistance. Karimganj is not just an administrative unit, it is a lived space, a borderland that carries the fragrance of Sylhet's folk tunes and the echoes of Barak's old ferry docks. It is this layered identity that the people sought to preserve.

Sociologists have long asserted that name changes are never neutral, they serve political objectives, reframe cultural memory, and often, erase inconvenient truths. In this case, renaming Karimganj to Sribhumi was seen by many as part of a broader ideological pattern that seeks to sanitize the Bengali-Muslim cultural influence of the Barak Valley under the guise of spiritual revivalism. The rejection, therefore, was not simply about nostalgia, it was about self-preservation.

The streets of Karimganj became places of discourse. Elders recalled stories of the first time they crossed over from Sylhet in 1947, of the warmth with which their new neighbors received them, and how the name Karimganj became a symbol of that welcoming continuity. Youth groups started recording these oral histories, planning to document the resistance through podcasts, pamphlets, and films.

In cafes and paan stalls, the conversations turned deeper. People wondered why Karimganj was renamed without consultation. They compared it to past instances where names of places had been altered, be it Allahabad to Prayagraj, or Gurgaon to Gurugram. But in those cases, at least some degree of public discourse preceded the change. Here, the announcement had come like a jolt, abrupt, opaque, and unilateral.

Even those who had no clear political leanings found themselves angered. "They say Sribhumi means sacred land. But this land was already sacred to us," said one boatman from Nilambazar. "Why not ask the ones who live here what it means to them?"

Despite all this, the government stood firm. No retraction was announced. But the people did not give up.

Months later, by mid-2025, protest vigils were still being held. Booklets compiling resistance essays, protest poems, and art from students were published and distributed across Barak Valley. The name Karimganj continued to be used in wedding invitations, property deeds, school certificates, and birth registrations. People did not wait for a legal order to continue their legacy, they lived it.

To this day, the word "Sribhumi" exists only in government files, signboards, and official documents. But in hearts, homes, and hushed lullabies, Karimganj remains.

Because a name is not just a word. It is a map of memory.

Let this chapter be that map. Let no reader ever forget: We are not Sribhumi. We are Karimganj. We are Sylheti.

XII
What They Wrote Before Us

"We are not the first to speak — only the ones who refuse to be forgotten."

Every story begins somewhere, and ours was never silent. Long before we picked up the pen, others had already begun sketching the contours of Barak Valley and Sylhet's shared legacy. The ink of earlier writers, poets, historians, and journalists still lingers in the air of our libraries, whispers in our school walls, and echoes in the dusty corners of old bookshops in Karimganj, Silchar, and Hailakandi. Before us, there were voices that had tried to describe the ache of partition, the smell of wet soil after river floods, and the resilience of a people often overlooked.

One cannot begin this chapter without acknowledging the legendary Syed Mujtaba Ali , born in Karimganj in 1904, he became a towering figure of Bengali literature. His works like *Deshe Bideshe* and *Panchatantra* reveal a wit and cosmopolitanism rarely matched, but within his words are also the faint scents of home, of borderless Barak, of the Sylhet he once knew. Mujtaba Ali was not just a writer, he was an archivist of memory, one who could laugh and bleed in the same sentence. His writing stands as a reminder that exile, both physical and emotional, leaves a mark that literature alone can carry forward. Through his works, he charted journeys, from Kabul to Calcutta, but his heart always returned to the banks of the Kushiyara.

In the pages of Dainik Nababarta Prasanga, Dainik Samayik Prasanga countless unnamed journalists brought regional concerns to the forefront. Week after week, they wrote about floods submerging schools, bridges left half-constructed, rising unemployment, smuggling across porous borders, and forgotten holidays. These writers often received no recognition. They never won awards. But they wrote because someone had to. Their articles built the bones of Barak's memory, a memory that the state often ignored.

And then, there were the anonymous writers, school teachers who wrote for local magazines, students who started campus newspapers, women who wrote letters to editors from behind veils. They wrote not for fame, but to breathe, to protest, to exist. Many of their works have been lost to time, but their echoes remain.

Today, when we write about Barak, its pain, pride, and peculiar politics, we walk on a path already paved by these predecessors. Their words are our foundation. Our books are built on their struggles. Their courage to write in times of indifference gave us permission to speak louder.

This chapter is not a bibliography. It is a remembrance. An offering. We do not claim to be the first, or the best. But we claim them as our lineage.

We carry their ink in our blood.

XIII
Barak Speaks in Many Tongues

The Hidden Languages of a Valley

They say a region is shaped by the tongues that move within it, but Barak Valley is not simply shaped, it is sung, whispered, protested, prayed, and dreamt into existence by a symphony of languages. Not all of them are written. Not all of them are spoken. Some lie beneath rivers, stitched into old prayer mats, or folded into a sari's pleats. Others are etched on boundary stones and tea leaves, in market haggling and classroom silences. Barak does not speak in one language, it speaks in echoes.

The first sound most children hear is not the cry of birth, but a lullaby. A mother in a hamlet of Karimganj, tired but tender, hums an old Sylheti tune: one she heard from her grandmother, who crossed from Sylhet during Partition with nothing but this song in her throat. The words may not make sense to a stranger, but to that child, they are grammar and galaxy. The lullaby teaches them belonging, a language older than alphabets.

Walk into a crowded alley near Hailakandi bazar and you'll hear a layered cacophony, one that would make any linguist pause. A tea seller speaks in a mix of Sylheti and Bishnupriya. A vegetable vendor answers in Assamese-laced Bengali. A group of migrant workers use a hybrid tongue born out of labour, necessity, and shared laughter. These are languages with no dictionaries, no spellings, only survival.

Every language in Barak Valley carries a memory. Sylheti carries the grief of separation, from Sylhet, from recognition, from inclusion. Bengali carries martyrdom, from 1961, from textbooks never rewritten. Urdu lingers in Friday sermons, in the calligraphy of graveyards. Hindi enters through Bollywood, education, and bureaucracy, foreign yet familiar. English arrives like a visitor wearing a coat in summer, respected, but not trusted.

Faith has its tongues too. In Barak, the mosque and the mandir often share a wall, and sometimes a silence. The azaan doesn't compete with the arati. Both rise into the same sky, echoing through temples in Katigorah and mosques in Badarpur, and sometimes heard together on community loudspeakers during festivals, not by design, but by destiny. It is a language of co-prayer.

There is a language of protest that Barak invented. Not always slogans, but poems. Not always marches, but murals. Not always anger, but aching. When Karimganj was renamed, the streets didn't erupt with violence, but with rhymes. "Not Sribhumi" wasn't just a chant, it was a lyric. In student unions, on WhatsApp statuses, in children's debates, the language of resistance bloomed like spring.

Even silence has a sound in Barak. The silence of tea garden workers when asked about their wages. The silence of the old man in Dullabcherra who hasn't heard from his Sylhet cousin since 1947. The silence of women who light lamps in both Durga Puja and Eid. The silence of a child in a class who doesn't speak fluent Bengali and gets laughed at, even though their soul sings in Sylheti.

Barak is not just a region of dialects. It is a confluence of layered linguistic identities. Sylheti is spoken in homes and hearts, rich in oral tradition, though not yet distinctly reflected in official language classifications. Bishnupriya carries centuries of cultural memory. Urdu adds spiritual resonance in prayers and poetry. Hindi and English serve educational and administrative bridges, connecting Barak to broader national dialogues. Every language here coexists, not in competition, but in harmony. Each voice is not an echo of division, but a thread in the shared fabric of Barak's multilingual soul.

In festivals, language turns visual. Look at the rickshaw puller's garland. The shop sign with three scripts. The rangoli made with river sand, spelling out "Ami Baraker Chele/Mey." In rituals, language becomes gesture. The way hands fold, the way turmeric is applied, the way prayers end with "Dua korben."

But most moving of all is the digital tongue Barak is learning. Youth on Instagram making reels in Sylheti. YouTubers teaching the world how "Oise" is different from "Hoyeche." Pages like Barak Kantha, Northeast Comedians, Kasabangla, Tipu Khan Entertainment, ERN Comedy, etc translating trauma into trends. Language is now viral. But even here, it remains local. No matter how many filters are added, the accent leaks through. The dialect dances.

Barak speaks in many tongues. and all of them resist erasure. This chapter will not attempt to list them all. It will simply let them breathe.

Because no one language defines us. And none of them should be lost.

The diaspora speaks too. When the children of Barak leave for London, Birmingham, or Dubai, they don't just carry suitcases, they carry sounds. A mother calling "Baba, odike aao," from the veranda, becomes a voice message saved forever. A wedding video of cousins dancing to a Sylheti hit song becomes their lullaby abroad.

These immigrants, born from soil and silence, recreate Barak in new cities, not just through food or festivals, but in language.

In Tower Hamlets or Queens, in Bur Dubai or Melbourne, you'll find shops named “Sylheti Spices,” “Barak Mart,” “Bondhur Dokan.” Their owners speak Bengali with a curve, Sylheti with a pause, English with a flare, and all three in the same sentence. Their children grow up saying “Ami home o jaiar,” without realizing they're speaking poetry.

Language doesn't die. It migrates. It mutates. It mingles. The tongue that was once laughed at in a Silchar classroom becomes a badge of pride in a café in Canada. The nickname “Bablu” becomes “Babloo” to a British classmate, but its emotional meaning remains intact. These transformations aren't loss. They are evolution.

And in the midst of this, are the food names, edible dictionaries of identity. Shutki, bharta, panta bhaat, doi-chira. Names that don't need translation, because they arrive at your nose before they reach your ears. Each dish speaks of rivers, seasons, harvests, and home. Recipes passed down in verbal shorthand: “ektu ekhane gorom masala dao,” is not a sentence, it's inheritance. A girl in Ontario, watching her grandmother on video call mix turmeric and salt into mustard oil, learns more about her homeland than any map could teach her.

In Barak, names are language too. Every name, even a pet name, carries layers. “Bappa,” “Munni,” “Chinku,” “Ranu,” “Moyna,” “Raju” — they're not just words, they're archives. Often given with a smile and never written down, they last longer than formal names.

Love has its own grammar here. Not all love letters are written. Some are in the way water is poured during a guest's visit. In the careful wrapping of tamarind in newspaper for a child. In the playful insult, "Tui amar matha noshto kori disos.".

Insults, too, are a form of language. Barak insults are witty, layered, and surprisingly poetic. "Tui amar matha kharap kori disos," "Gorur moto pagol oiso," "Matha nai tor, shudhu much," "Tumar brain monehoy hatut." They are cultural performances, not just fights. In fact, arguments in Barak are more theatrical than aggressive. They involve rhythm, rhyme, repetition. People don't just shout, they compose.

Code-switching isn't only a modern invention here. It has existed in every household where a mother speaks in Sylheti, the father replies in Bengali, the child responds in English, and the grandmother watches silently, her language unspoken but understood. Generations in Barak live in multilinguality without effort. It's not a skill, it's survival.

Language also hides in rituals, small, seemingly trivial things. The way we touch elders' feet and say "Dua korba," even if we barely believe. The way we end phone calls with "Bhalo thakis." These phrases are not just manners. They are prayerful punctuation.

Some people never got to speak their language aloud. Grandfathers who couldn't read Sylheti because it wasn't taught. Tea garden workers whose tribal dialects remain undocumented. Widows who spoke only in gesture after their husbands passed. Their silence is not emptiness, it is a story waiting to be told.

The language of loss is quiet, but heavy. It echoes in empty prayer rooms, in unvisited graves, in the black-and-white photo albums no one opens anymore. It says: we were here. We spoke. We sang. Even if no one recorded us.

And yet, there is hope. Every time a child learns a Sylheti joke. Every time someone from Karimganj starts a YouTube channel. Every time an immigrant tears up hearing “Bondhu amar roila re.” Hope lives in these sounds. Not in museums, but in mouths.

Barak’s language is not linear. It loops. It skips. It comes back after decades. A lost phrase returns in a festival. A forgotten word appears in a dream. It’s like the river: sometimes calm, sometimes flooding, but always flowing.

The river doesn’t ask permission to speak. Neither does Barak.

In Barak, language is not just survival; it is celebration. It lives in the rhythm of daily life. At the fish market in Karimganj, the calls of the vendors form their own melody, “Ilish lo, Ilish,” sung louder with every passing customer. At tea gardens, laughter breaks out in bursts, mixing tribal dialects with Sylheti jokes. The women there have their own codes, their own playful gestures that say more than a sentence ever could.

Every festival in Barak brings a new burst of vocabulary. During Durga Puja, one hears Sanskrit chants flowing side by side with street-side banter in Bengali. On Eid, homes echo with greetings like “Eid mubarak bhai, dawaat roilo biryanir,” and neighbors laugh across fences. During Christmas, the churches fill with songs in Assamese,

Bengali, English, sometimes all in one hymn. Languages blend not because they must, but because they want to.

Children invent their own versions of language, a mix of what they hear on YouTube, at school, and in the kitchen. One moment they are reciting an English rhyme, the next moment they ask their Dida/Dadi, "Doi aachhe?" That blend, that shift, is effortless. It is not confusion, it is creativity. Their notebooks may be in English, but their hearts whisper in the tongue of home.

In every family, there is a different language of love. A grandfather who says "Ektu cha banai bay ni?" isn't just asking for tea, he's asking for company. A mother who shouts "Ghor e ja!" isn't angry, she's worried. A brother who says "Pagol ni tui?" isn't being rude, he's being affectionate. These are not insults or commands; they are caring, wrapped in sound.
Songs are perhaps the most joyful form of language. Sylheti songs — romantic, humorous, devotional, still play on loudspeakers during weddings, fairs, and harvests. "Noya Daman, Beni Khuley, Rangabati" becomes the anthem of a celebration. Children dance, elders smile, and everyone, regardless of age, knows the lyrics. These songs need no formal translation, their rhythm is universal.

In Barak, people speak with their hands too. A raised eyebrow means curiosity. A tap on the shoulder says "Let's go." A wave from a rickshaw driver to a familiar face is more expressive than a hello. Even silence carries warmth, a neighbor sitting beside you in the evening without speaking is still saying, "I am here."

Food is a language all its own. The way someone serves rice first shows hospitality. The offer of a second helping of fish curry says, "You are family." A spoon of gur after a meal, shared without asking, says, “Stay a little longer.” These gestures are not taught in school. They are taught by generations, passed through kitchens and courtyards.

Barak speaks in smells too. The smell of mustard oil in the morning, of incense during puja, of earth after the rain. These aromas are part of memory, part of language. They remind us of belonging, of being from somewhere that matters.

There is joy in Barak’s many tongues, a kind of music made from the harmony of difference. It’s in how a Manipuri song and a Sylheti dance can happen on the same stage during college fest. How a group of school friends joke in three languages at once. How someone from Dullabcherra and someone from Silchar can instantly understand each other, not just through words, but through tone, timing, and shared laughter.

This is a valley where no language is ever truly lost. Even the forgotten words return, sometimes in dreams, sometimes in stories told before bedtime. Sometimes in a wedding song that no one knows the origin of, but everyone knows the meaning.

Language in Barak is not a tool. It is a tradition. It is a tapestry, constantly being woven by its people, in joy, in friendship, in ritual, and in rhythm.

Barak’s language dances on stage as well. Folk theatre and natok (plays) have long been mediums of expression here, humorous, dramatic, and musical. During festivals in Banskandi or Katlicherra, you’ll see open-air performances where dialogue moves between Sylheti and Hindi, with comic lines thrown in English. The audience laughs not because they understand every word, but because they feel every pause. Intonation becomes punchline. Familiar characters speak for the entire village.

Every festival has its own soundscape. During Rath Yatra, you hear conch shells, "Jay Jagannath" chants, and teenage volunteers shouting instructions. During Eid, families greet neighbors in a dozen tones of "Eid Mubarak," often mixed with wishes in English. On Christmas, choirs rehearse carols that blend Hindi verses with Bengali chorus. Barak does not choose between traditions, it layers them like a well-made meal.

Even sporting events become multilingual festivals. A football final between two towns becomes a ground of roaring phrases, playful threats, and cheerleader chants that blend Bengali, Sylheti, and tribal shouts. Players might argue in one tongue and celebrate in another. And when the trophy is handed over, no language is needed, only applause.

There's also a new generation of artists who express Barak's voice visually. Digital creators are using phrases like "Ki khobor?" and "Boro bondhu" as brand slogans. These aren't just memes, they're preservation through pixels.

You'll find poets in Barak who publish their work on Instagram, using a mix of three scripts in one stanza, Bengali, Roman, and even emoji. This may confuse purists, but it represents exactly what Barak is: a mosaic. Their verses read like musical notes, unbound, unrestricted, and unashamed of being many things at once.

Even weather has a tongue here. The first clap of thunder is greeted with "Kal boishakhi aar." The first drizzle makes someone say "Bhaat or scent pailam." Children learn these phrases without being taught. These are not meteorological statements, they are emotional readings of the sky.

There are songs sung only during harvest. Chants used only while applying mehendi. Proverbs whispered before exams. Compliments that sound like scoldings. Warnings delivered like blessings. Wishes spoken as metaphors. Every aspect of life in Barak has a voice.

We see a future where this voice grows louder, prouder. Where it is not just preserved, but celebrated. Where Barak's many tongues don't whisper in fear but sing in freedom.

Language in Barak is not past. It is potential. It is presence.
And it is endless.

A new era is arriving where language is no longer confined to mouths and memories, it's typed, streamed, posted, and archived. In Barak Valley, youth are building platforms that echo the sound of home. One click on a video and a familiar accent fills the screen. "Ei kun style re, bhai!" someone says, and suddenly, a million viewers know what it means to be from Barak. The accent that once drew giggles now draws followers.

Young musicians remix old Sylheti songs with electronic beats. Spoken word poets upload their verses to Spotify. This is not nostalgia, this is movement. A graphic designer from Silchar is creating stickers for messaging apps with local expressions. "Ki moja re" and "Tui amar bhai" now exist not just in hearts, but on screens.

What was once passed by memory is now getting metadata. Lullabies are being recorded. Recipes are becoming eBooks. Dialects are being digitally mapped. A grandmother's prayer is now a podcast episode. A child's rhyme is now a ringtone. The valley is not just speaking, it is being documented.

The dream is larger. Imagine a Barak Language Archive, a digital museum of every dialect, idiom, and folk phrase. Audio stories, scanned manuscripts, village plays, childhood rhymes, greetings from across generations. A place where language lives forever, not just for Barak, but for the world to see what resilience sounds like.

Language in Barak is not just about identity. It is about joy. About community. About play. It teaches us not who we are, but how we belong. It tells a child that their voice matters, even if it's different. It tells a grandmother that her song still lives. It tells the world that being multilingual is not a burden, it's a gift.

Every lane, every prayer, every festival in Barak carries a new word waiting to be heard. And if we listen closely, we'll find that the valley has always been speaking, not just in one language, but in a hundred harmonies.

We do not need to choose one tongue to call home. Because in Barak Valley, every tongue is home.

And that is our legacy, not just to protect, but to sing.

There is a quiet revolution happening in living rooms and courtyards, where grandparents become memory keepers.

Elders gather children around during load-shedding nights and share stories that begin with "A long time ago, when the Kushiyara ran fuller..." These tales, half-truths and full-wonder, often don't make it into textbooks, but they live in language. And not just in Bengali, but in the creole forms, in playful suffixes, in dramatic tones that children come to cherish.

In every mohalla (locality) of Barak, there's always that one person, the local jester, the wedding announcer, the schoolteacher with twenty catchphrases, whose use of language is performance art. They are the archive in human form. They preserve not only stories, but the way those stories are told. Their sentences include claps, whistles, laughter, pauses. They remind us that orality is not just an older form of literature, it is literature.

In Barak, language is also shaped by movement. Boatmen use hand signals and water calls. Market vendors use nicknames instead of product names. "Momo Bappon Da?" is all that's said, and a stall owner already knows which mustard oil brand is meant. The economy runs not just on rupees, but on linguistic shorthand, built over generations of shared memory.

Children imitate this without realizing. They create games with made-up syllables, assign secret meanings to regular words. A group of friends might use "moi" to mean something entirely different from its usual context, like a code language of loyalty. These invented forms are as valid as any institutional language. In fact, they're more alive.

Temples and mosques have their own registers. At pujas, mantras are chanted in Sanskrit, but the commentary is in Bengali or Sylheti. At mosques, khutbahs are in Arabic, but discussions afterward shift seamlessly to the local dialect. Language in Barak is sacred, but it is also social. It's never static, it adapts to context with grace.

In weddings, announcements are made in rhyme. “gate e taka deu ar bou nau” a playful line to welcome the groom’s party. In funerals, whispers of old blessings and hymns are passed like warm cloth in winter. Even in grief, there is beauty in how words are shared.

Libraries in Barak are now rethinking their role. Some have started collecting oral histories, recording local elders, scanning hand-written notebooks, preserving pamphlets from the 1970s. Young volunteers are going house to house, asking people to share family phrases, recipes, local riddles. These projects are not academic, they are intimate. It is language conservation with a heartbeat..

Language in Barak is carried not only by people, but by nature. The rustle of bamboo in rain, the chorus of frogs during flood season, the chirp of birds at dawn, all have phrases attached. “Brishti aibo,” someone says after a specific birdcall. These observations are not scientific, yet accurate. Language doesn’t describe nature here it interprets it.

Mobile applications are starting to include Sylheti phrases for translation. Voice AI assistants can now recognize “Ki khobor?” and “Ami ekhane asi.” Students are building keyboard overlays to text in their own dialect. Tech is finally catching up to the tongues that never went silent.

Everywhere in Barak, a sense of linguistic ownership is emerging. No longer shy, no longer seen as “less than,” the local speech patterns are becoming a matter of pride. College students proudly deliver project presentations with Sylheti phrases. Content creators introduce themselves with "Baraker chele" or "Hailakandir takia koiar." There is a musicality in this rootedness.

To speak in Barak Valley is to sing without instruments. To listen in Barak is to read without paper. To belong in Barak is to feel language in every season, every smile, every shared moment.

No chapter, no archive, no documentary can contain the full soundscape of this valley. But together, word by word, voice by voice, we build something that lasts.

And as long as we keep speaking, even softly, Barak will never be forgotten.

Language moves with rhythm, and in Barak, rhythm moves everything. There's a beat to how people speak here. From the rising intonations of street hawkers in Hailakandi to the soothing, drawn-out vowels of a lullaby in Badarpur, the tone carries the emotion even when the words change. In many homes, grandparents still tell the time not by clocks, but by what birds are singing. "Shokaler pakkhi gelo," they say, as a way of saying morning has come. That is the language of lived wisdom.

Farmers read the earth like they read a newspaper. They listen to the language of soil, of wind, of rustling trees. Children are taught these observations not in textbooks, but by walking through the paddy fields with their elders. These expressions are ecological literacy embedded in everyday speech.

In marriages and festivals, humour is a key ingredient. Barak's wedding MCs don't just announce they perform. Puns, jokes, clever rhymes, all delivered in perfectly timed local dialects, get the entire crowd roaring. These aren't just speeches — they're linguistics in celebration. Language becomes theatre, and the community becomes its audience.

There's a growing trend among Barak's creative youth, inserting regional phrases into English essays, blogs, even résumés. A student might write, "I'm a proud Silcharian, fluent in Sylheti, and never say 'no' to shutki." These aren't errors, they are identity statements. This playful defiance reclaims dignity without confrontation.

It's not just human language that matters here. The dialect of festivals includes colour, food, sound, and scent. The smell of nolen gur announces winter more clearly than any calendar. The sound of dhol during Bihu reminds even a sleeping child that joy has arrived. Even the firecrackers during Diwali carry a vocabulary of excitement.

The music of Barak itself is a dictionary. From "Tomay Hridh Majare Rakhbo" to "Oporadhi" and "Tunir Maa," "Shundori Maiyya," "Moner Manush," "Dekha Na Dile, Kotha Koiyo Na," the songs act as cultural time capsules. Lyrics preserve idioms, inflections, and cultural humour.

Slogans, too, are linguistic markers. Protest lines like "Bhashar lagiya rokto dite parmu" echo alongside love slogans like "Tui amar basha." Whether for politics or passion, the choice of words reflects the emotional landscape of a community that loves hard and speaks louder..

It's not about purity. It's about presence. A Sylheti sentence mixed with English and peppered with emoji still counts. A family WhatsApp group where elders type in Roman and youth reply in voice notes is still a community of language. What matters is that the bridge remains intact.

Some words in Barak cannot be translated. Not fully. “Thanda thanda lage” is not just about temperature it’s a feeling. “Dukkho oilo” isn’t merely sorrow, it’s soft empathy. “Aish koro” isn’t just welcome, it’s an embrace. These words are culture in capsule form.
And so, to speak in Barak is to carry history in your throat, music in your breath, and affection in your grammar. It is to belong, not just to a geography, but to a memory.

As we approach the close of this chapter, we find that there is no close at all. Barak’s languages don’t end with a full stop. They continue, in laughter, in lullabies, in long phone calls between cousins, in messages sent home from abroad, in roadside greetings, in classroom jokes.

They live.
They bloom.
And they carry us forward.

When a new life begins in Barak Valley, language is the first gift it receives. A child born in a Karimganj clinic might hear blessings whispered in three languages before sunset. A lullaby in Sylheti, a verse from scripture, a joke from a cousin in broken English. This is not confusion, this is heritage wrapped in melody.

From the very beginning, language in Barak is not taught as rule, it is lived as ritual. It’s in how the newborn is held, how food is tasted, how footsteps are echoed. There’s no need for formal grammar here; rhythm and warmth are enough.

Language defines how we greet and how we part. “Dua Roilo” is not just a farewell, it’s a lingering blessing. “Ki khobor?” can mean everything from “How are you?” to “I missed you." One phrase, depending on tone, can ask a question or express love. In Barak, intonation is meaning.

Even the way we joke is shaped by language. Barak's humour is self-deprecating, tender, and sharp. "Ami toh Baraker shutki khawra manus," someone might say when called fancy, folding pride into a smile. Jokes often begin with "Shuncho, ekta kotha koi," and end with laughter that needs no translation.

Our festivals continue this flow of feeling. During Magh Bihu, food becomes language. During Eid, hospitality becomes syntax. During Christmas, togetherness is the script. Every celebration adds new idioms to our lexicon, words that carry memories, seasons, and scents.

Schools are beginning to teach students how to collect these phrases from their elders. A project called "Dadu'r Kotha" pairs students with grandparents, asking them to write down favorite sayings. From "Bhalo hoy jodi bhalo thako" to "Mon kharap, mangsho lagbo," these expressions are being archived, not to be fossilized, but to be cherished.

In the world of technology, Barak's youth are crafting keyboards and sticker packs with local phrases. Emojis are now paired with "Maiggo!" and "Ja re bondhu!" It is not mockery, it is movement..

The world has become curious too. Researchers, bloggers, and travelers arrive asking, "What does this word mean?" They are welcomed not with definitions, but with stories. Because in Barak, every word has a home, and every home has a history.

Language lives in love stories. The shy proposal whispered behind school walls. The handwritten letter where Bengali curls into Sylheti confessions. The wedding song where every stanza is a promise. These expressions may never be published, but they are spoken into eternity.

And what about the names? The names we give, the ones we inherit. Names like Moyna, Faruk, Rina, Nirmal, each carrying meanings shaped by rivers and rebels, by saints and seasons. Names are never just sounds. They are claims to identity. They say: I am of Barak Valley.

In our diaspora, language becomes a bridge home. A mother in Kuwait plays old Barak songs while cooking. A student in Delhi changes their ringtone to "Tunir Maa." A taxi driver in Mumbai hears "Tumar bari koi ba?" and suddenly knows he is not alone. Language is not just sound, it is solace.

We are reaching a time where Sylheti might not only be spoken, but officially recognized. Campaigns for language recognition are growing. Linguists are researching Barak's dialects with respect. Slowly, the official silence around us is being replaced with applause.

In closing, there is no one way to describe the voice of Barak. It is layered, loving, laughing, and alive. It doesn't seek permission to exist. It doesn't need translation to be valid. It is a living script, handwritten in daily life.

So let us speak. Let us listen. Let us write. Let us remember.

And let Barak continue to speak in all its glorious tongues, because in its language, we find our home.

XIV
The Vision: What Barak Valley Deserves

"We have inherited a struggle — but we dream of a future."

The hourglass has emptied on our old grievances, but in its wake, we must fill our hands with vision, clear, courageous, and unignorable. Because a valley that fought for its voice cannot settle for whispers. And so, as you read this chapter, know it is not polemic, it is prophecy. It is a conversation with the land, a promise to the future.

It begins with an airport. Silchar's long-awaited greenfield airport at Doloo tea estate – cement, steel, and runway, promises to begin construction on December 1, 2025, under the Centre's Gati Shakti initiative, at a cost of approximately ₹1,455 crore. For years, wave after wave of hope has crashed against the walls of delay, but now, those walls will come down. Far more than simply linking air to land, this airport is our symbolic lifeline to connectivity with the rest of India, to economic revival, and to self-worth. Nearly 800 voices rose in the public hearing, 95 percent in favor, but some 1,296 families from Doloo tea estate still await clarity on rehabilitation after the uprooting of 42 lakh tea bushes. Their questions are our questions, of fairness, of modernization that lifts and does not crush.

We will not allow an airport to bloom with one voice silent. Its runways must carry our dreams, not only of travel, but of equitable development, livelihoods restored, ecological responsibility, and a true bridge between valleys and generations. Construction must involve genuine consultations, fair resettlement, employment guarantees, sustainability measures, to be an airport for all, not a spectacle for some.

But what happens when planes land? Where will people go? How will they breathe if hospitals choke, or students float through an academic abyss? Silchar Medical College, founded in 1960 and permanently established in 1968 as one of North East India's earliest government medical colleges, remains our only medical college in Barak Valley. It handles over 800 beds and is the lone tertiary referral center, serving complex regions across Assam, Mizoram, Tripura, Manipur, and Meghalaya. Its Department of Surgery alone treats around 50,000 patients annually, performing nearly 3,000 major operations. It admits over 100 MBBS and 71 postgraduate students, supported by 172 faculty members.

Yet, behind these numbers are halls of suffering. Patients from far-flung corners queue in dusty corridors. Students and doctors juggle resources, pediatricians fill wards meant for adult medicine, and lecture halls double as impromptu clinics. When floods struck in June 2025, the college and organising teams ran 487 medical camps, treating over 7,200 patients across Cachar and Kitagor areas. These emergency efforts, while praiseworthy, underscore the chronic shortage of medical infrastructure in towns like Karimganj and Hailakandi. The future demands not one, but several medical colleges, some already announced in the 2025 State Budget, but their materialisation remains unfulfilled.

We envision hospitals with multi-specialty wings, trauma centers, digital health records, and community field clinics evenly spread across Barak Valley. A valley that airs hope must also heal hope.

Education is next. Beyond medicine, we need universities where students can study Sylheti language, Barak history, folk arts, environment, and infrastructure. Institutions where researchers compile oral histories, river studies, tea ecology. Where young poets, artists, engineers, and entrepreneurs find roots and wings in the same ground.

Where a student from Panchgram can study agro-processing, a child from Ujandihi can explore freedom history, and a girl from Hailakandi can become a hybrid skilled in climate sciences and musical heritage.

Recall the Sylheti songs in the previous chapter, the sky of tradition that weaved through wedding processions and Youtube channels. We must archive them in public repositories. Build theatre spaces where plays can stage our stories unchanged. Record songs of the boatmen and matriarchs. Affirm that our languages Sylheti, Tripuri, Manipuri, are not relics, they are living.

We see agro-industries where paper mills rise again with sustainable fiber from bamboo and kenaf. Tea gardens like Hilara, Hatikhira, Aylabari must become organic cooperatives with fair trade certification, not monocultures of despair. Sand banks in Kushiyara and

Infrastructure calls for flood-resilient roads, year-round railway links, and all-weather bridges. Flight connectivity must extend to Delhi, Mumbai, and Bengaluru. not just to caterers and migrants, but business persons, educators, healthcare seekers, and diaspora visitors.

Above all, we deserve unity. Where Hindus and Muslims, Bengalis and Manipuris, Sylhetis and Dimasa, recall 1961 not to divide but as warning. Where floods do not differentiate, and elections rally human dignity. Where Barak Valley becomes a model of plural resilience, not a footnote of neglect.

This is not utopia. It is claim. It is plan.
Written in rice husks and runway concrete, in study halls and clinic wards, this chapter is not question, it is demand. Barak Valley deserves nothing less.

XV
Kingdoms That Ruled Barak Valley

The land we now call Barak Valley did not emerge with one ruler's decree, nor under one kingdom's flag. It was formed through centuries of passage, power, resistance, surrender, and survival. It is a story not written in one language, nor sealed in a single archive. Its story is told in rivers that changed course, in ruins hidden beneath tea gardens, in last names inherited from Mughal sanads, in temple bells and the call of azaan echoing together in the same valley. It was never truly ruled by anyone, not completely because this valley, this breathing stretch of land, always whispered something different back to those who tried to possess it: that belonging is earned, not taken.

Before kings arrived, there were clans. Before alphabets were carved into copper plates, there were chants around forest fires, and barter among riverbanks. The earliest known settlements in what is today the Barak Valley likely belonged to tribes whose names we may never fully know. The valley's geography, bordered by lush hills to the south and east, watered by rivers that flowed like arteries of trade and life, made it fertile, strategic, and desirable. The earliest rulers did not come with crowns, but with kinship and control over rivers.

Historians agree that by the 4th century CE, Barak Valley was part of the Kamarupa kingdom, a vast and spiritually rich domain that extended from the Brahmaputra basin down into parts of modern-day Sylhet. It was a kingdom of Sanskritized royalty, of early Hindu influence, of temples dedicated to Shiva and Kamakhya. Kamarupa's legacy wasn't only political. It laid the foundation of ritual life, early landholding practices, and mythological reverence across Assam and beyond. While its court language was Sanskrit, the people spoke in many tongues. And Barak, even then, was a tongue of its own.

The Kamarupa rulers, from the Varman to the Pala dynasties, did not directly administer every inch of the Barak plains. Rather, they influenced them through regional lords and alliances. The valley was a mosaic of forest kingdoms and settled tribes, whose allegiance was often fluid. But temples were built. Copper plate inscriptions have been found in nearby regions referring to grants of land, suggesting that the Barak landscape was already sacred, already storied.

When Kamarupa began to fragment, a vacuum opened, and Bengal moved in. From the west, the Gauda Kingdom (Gour) under the Sena rulers extended their cultural and administrative hand into Sylhet and Karimganj. With Bengal came the Bengali language in its early form, Vaishnavism, caste stratification, and a new system of feudal governance. The Pala dynasty, a Buddhist revivalist force in Bengal, also left spiritual footprints, faint, but persistent, in this borderland. Many shrines in the valley today reflect mixed influences: Hindu symbols, Islamic architecture, and tribal customs. These are not contradictions, they are historical residues.

The Tripura kings from the south came not just as rulers, but as protectors of hills and patrons of local deities. Their influence over parts of Hailakandi and the Barail range left behind more than tax routes, it shaped the memory of the hills. Even today, some tribal communities in the inner Barak districts trace their customs to Tripura's Manikya dynasty. These kings sent emissaries, collected tributes, and negotiated alliances through marriages and land-sharing. The valley was never fully theirs, but they knew better than to ignore it.

By the 14th century, Islamic rule in Bengal began expanding eastward. The Sultans of Bengal, led by rulers like Shamsuddin Firoz Shah, sent military expeditions into Sylhet, capturing it in 1303 with the spiritual and tactical leadership of Hazrat Shah Jalal (R:). While Shah Jalal's influence remained centered in Sylhet, the wave he brought, of faith, of Sufism, of Persianate governance, lapped at the banks of Barak. It did not drown the older traditions. It merely layered over them.

And thus began a dual spiritual legacy, of ancient temples and new khanqahs, of Sanskrit slokas and Sufi qawwalis, coexisting, arguing, harmonizing. Barak Valley became one of the few regions where a Mughal faujdar's fort stood within sight of a Shaivite shrine. Where a Dewan's palace kept both a Quran and a Bhagavad Gita in its library. Where names like Choudhury, Laskar, Bhattacharjee, and Syed came to represent not divisions, but chapters in a continuous book.

When the Mughals rose to prominence in northern India and reached eastern Bengal, their administrators naturally turned their eyes toward the riverine wealth and geo political significance of Barak Valley. The Mughals were not only empire builders but master bureaucrats, their true strength lay in how well they measured, recorded, and taxed the land. In 1612 AD, parts of Karimganj and adjoining Sylhet came under Mughal governance. The area was placed under the jurisdiction of faujdars, military governors who oversaw law, order, and revenue collection. Land grants, or sanads, were issued to trustworthy individuals and influential families, many of whom still carry Mughal-appointed titles to this day. Names like Dewan Arman Ali Choudhury trace their origins to such appointments.

The Mughals did not impose through destruction in Barak. They ruled with documents and deals. They offered rewards in exchange for loyalty. They surveyed land not to bless it, but to price it. Families were empowered through zamindari rights, making them intermediaries between imperial tax officers and local cultivators. This system embedded a new class, educated, literate, often bilingual, fluent in both Persian and Bengali, into the valley's fabric. They became the custodians of knowledge and influence, bridging ancient oral wisdom with imperial written law.

But no rule is forever. As the Mughal Empire weakened, the valley began to reassert its local rhythm. In the early 19th century, the Dimasa Kingdom, centered in Khaspur near Silchar, emerged as the final indigenous monarchy of Barak. The Dimasas, an ethnic group with deep roots in the region, ruled with relative autonomy. Their kingdom was small compared to the Mughals, but deeply rooted in the land and forest. King Gobinda Chandra, the last Dimasa monarch, maintained a complex relationship with the British East India Company. After his assassination in 1830, the British annexed Cachar, marking the end of independent royal rule in the Barak Valley.

With the arrival of British colonialism, everything changed, not only governance but identity. The British brought roads and railways, tea estates and post offices, schools and administrative divisions. But more than that, they brought a way of classifying people and places that disconnected them from their own histories. Barak Valley was first part of Bengal Presidency, then transferred to Assam Province in 1874, a political decision that would cause unrest, confusion, and linguistic wounds for the next century.

While British maps drew boundaries, British boats travelled the Barak River, carrying goods and imperial ambition. Tea plantations bloomed, while forests shrank.

Schools taught English, while local languages struggled for status. Zamindars now answered to district collectors. The names of the rulers were now European, Major Jenkins, Commissioner Playfair, Judge Higgins, and yet, they were never loved or remembered like the ones who ruled from within.

Through all of this, the people of Barak adapted, but never forgot. They remembered the Mughals who granted land and honored their family names. They remembered the Tripura kings whose emissaries brought news and trade. They remembered the Dimasas who governed from the heart of the valley. And they even remembered the British, but not always with bitterness, sometimes with a quiet sigh at how things were both broken and built in their time.

Empires may collapse, and kings may vanish into the fog of forgotten dynasties, but what remains are customs, rituals, and words. Barak Valley, more than being ruled by political centers, has been shaped by spiritual movements and cultural inheritances left behind by every ruler who passed through. Each kingdom, Hindu, Muslim, tribal, colonial, left more than borders. They left stories, shrines, and songs.

The temples of the Kamarupa era, now often rebuilt or reduced to foundations, were once the sanctums of social life. Many villages in Hailakandi and Silchar still house deities believed to be worshipped since ancient times, not just as gods, but as ancestral protectors. The spread of Shaivism and Shaktism in this valley owes much to those early dynasties. The land is still sacred not because it was ruled by pious kings, but because the people kept their piety through seasons of rule and rebellion.

When the Sultans of Bengal and Mughal governors brought Islam, they didn't bring only power, they brought saints. Sufism, which entered Sylhet through Hazrat Shah Jalal and his companions, spread through love, not war. The dargahs in Bishkut, Badarpur, Karimganj, and Silchar are not just religious sites, they are memories of a different kind of rule: one of spiritual equality, of divine access, of shared food and common grief. These shrines became gathering places for both Hindus and Muslims, and they remain so. Even today, many Hindu families in the Barak Valley still light candles at dargahs. Some do it for wishes, others for tradition, and some quietly because they always have.

The Tripura kings brought along not only political reach but syncretic tribal customs. Their worship of deities like Chandi, their reverence of forests, and their diplomacy with hill communities helped maintain Barak as a plural landscape. In Hailakandi's remote areas, one can still find hybrid rituals, blending tribal nature reverence with Puranic deities, passed down through generations.

Then came the British, who were not builders of temples or shrines, but of schools, post offices, and courtrooms. And yet, their impact on culture was profound. Missionary schools introduced English, but also created a new class of intellectuals, children of zamindars and farmers who now read Wordsworth and wrote in Bengali. The churches of Church Road in Karimganj and the convent schools in Silchar are not just colonial leftovers. They are testaments to the fact that Barak adapted, not blindly, but selectively. The people took what served them and reshaped what didn't.

Still, kingdoms did not only rule over land, they ruled over words and languages. The Mughals brought Persian into courtrooms. The British enforced English in schools. The Bengalis kept Sylheti alive in kitchens and lullabies. The Assamese administration, post-Independence, tried to introduce its own linguistic rhythm. And through all this, the valley refused to forget its mother tongue, Sylheti. This is perhaps Barak's strongest resistance: that no matter who ruled, the people kept speaking in their own way, often in a tongue the rulers didn't fully understand.

In markets and mosques, in temples and tea stalls, the echoes of these rulers live on, not in banners or statues, but in how people speak, how they greet each other, how they name their children, how they pray. You hear Arabic names with Sanskrit surnames, Bengali food with Tripuri spice, British schooling with Mughal manners. And that is Barak's greatest rebellion: it absorbed kingdoms, but never surrendered to any of them.

Even though thrones have turned to ruins and the names of kings have faded from calendars, the idea of rule has not entirely disappeared from Barak Valley. It has simply
changed costume. Today, the valley is not ruled by monarchs or faujdars or British commissioners. It is ruled by administrators, political parties, education boards, and media narratives. But the ghosts of the kingdoms still walk through these corridors, not haunting, but influencing.

In post-independence India, Barak Valley became part of the state of Assam, not by cultural choice, but by political geography. The rulers this time were no longer dynasties, but governments based in Dispur or Delhi, and often distant in temperament and tone. And though there are no swords or seals anymore, the people of Barak Valley still experience a kind of rule: one of language policies, budget allocations, forgotten roads, and imposed narratives.

When the state of Assam tried to enforce Assamese as the official language in the 1960s, the people of Barak rose not as rebels, but as heirs to a long tradition of cultural autonomy. They protested in the streets of

Silchar not because they were anti-Assamese, but because they had learned from centuries of rule that identity must be protected, not gifted by rulers, but preserved by the people. Eleven martyrs died during the 1961 language movement, but they did not die to create a kingdom. They died to remind the state that Barak's soul speaks differently, and that speech is not just sound, it is history.

Even in educational institutions, the legacy of previous rulers is visible. British-era schools still stand in Karimganj and Silchar. The syllabus still reflects a Bengali literary bias, a colonial historical lens, and a regional under-representation. The Dimasa kings who once ruled Khaspur are barely mentioned. Mughal sanads issued to local nobles rarely make it into history books. The Tripura-Assam-Bangladesh historical triad of Barak is seldom taught, even though every person in the valley carries some fragment of it in their bloodline or family story.

Politically too, the ghosts of past kingdoms hover. The Zamindari class, born during Mughal and British rule, still yields informal influence in local decisions, sometimes in panchayats, sometimes in legal disputes, and often in cultural leadership. Families that once owned land during the empire now run schools, clinics, or NGOs. The reverence they command is not just about what they do today, it is about the memory they carry. People still speak of surnames like "Choudhury," "Dewan," or "Syed" not merely as names, but as reminders of a past where leadership came with responsibility and recordkeeping.

But there is a modern kind of ruler too: the bureaucracy. In some ways, the most enduring kingdom to ever govern Barak has been the file. The office. The nod. The clearance. From road repairs to hospital funding, Barak's experience of rule has shifted from palaces to paper. And often, this governance feels distant and bureaucratic, rather than intimate and invested. The rulers of today do not live in the valley, and perhaps do not fully understand it. They arrive on surveys, stay for speeches, and leave behind promises, rarely blueprints.

And so, the valley continues to live in a state of silent negotiation. With memory. With governance. With development. And above all, with the question: Who do we belong to? The answer is complicated. Barak has belonged to many. But perhaps more importantly, many have belonged to Barak. Each ruler may have stamped their rule on maps, coins, or laws, but it is the land that left the lasting mark on them.

Even today, the everyday rhythm of life in Barak Valley is filled with remnants of old rule. A grandmother recites a Persian dua before giving turmeric milk. A family in Karimganj still uses the British name "Station Road," even though the signs have changed. A temple fair near Hailakandi includes Tripuri dance and Sylheti music. A college student reads Tagore in the morning, speaks Sylheti in the afternoon, and watches Delhi debates in the evening, moving seamlessly between centuries of influence.

And that is what makes Barak Valley so difficult to understand from outside, and so impossible to forget from within. It was never just ruled by kings. It was ruled by flows of culture, by language, by ancestry, by resistance, and by memory. Each of these rulers left something behind, but none could take everything with them. And that, perhaps, is Barak's final victory.

No empire ends with thunder. Most dissolve in silence. What remains is the land, carrying footprints that no ruler can erase. In Barak Valley, where three districts breathe under one sky, kingdoms have come and gone. But none have left unnoticed. Their memory is not preserved in grand museums or marble plaques. It lives in daily life, quiet, invisible, but enduring.

A walk through a quiet street in Karimganj tells more than any textbook. You pass a tea stall named after a forgotten faujdar. You see an old house with Mughal-style arches, now painted blue and green, its family unaware of the Persian symmetry carved into its bricks. In Hailakandi, a village priest recites mantras that trace back to when Kamarupa kings gave land to temple caretakers. In Silchar, the name of a road, once called "Station Road", survives colonial memory, even if the station itself has been rebuilt three times since.

Many do not know the names of the rulers who once claimed their homes. But they carry their legacies in rituals and rhythm. A wedding ceremony in Barak is rarely just one tradition. It's a blend. There's the Tripuri music, the Bengali attire, the Mughal feast, the British punctuality, all tied into one celebration. No one claims this as royal heritage. It's simply Barak's way.

Even the food tells history. The way mustard is used, or the preference for ghee in certain districts, or the sweetmeats served during festivals, all of it points to centuries of exchange. The markets may no longer sell goods under royal banners, but they still carry names: "Fatak Bazar", " Lala Bazar", "Mission Road" phrases carried forward not because of reverence, but because nobody ever renamed them.

And there are stories, told not in books but over warm rice and fish curry. A great-grandmother whispers about how her grandfather rode to Sylhet to pay tax to a Mughal-appointed zamindar. A tailor speaks of how his family stitched garments for a British officer who loved Sylheti tea. A schoolteacher remembers how his village held onto Bengali textbooks even after the border changed, not out of defiance, but out of habit, out of love. Children may not know the history of Gobinda Chandra or the Manikyas or the Mughal faujdars. But they walk on the same earth. They drink from wells dug during those times. They worship at temples and dargahs that outlived those kings.

They write poems in Sylheti, a language never officially ruled, but always spoken.

In the end, the valley does not remember its rulers through rebellion or resistance. It remembers them through retention. Through names that never faded, rituals that adapted, and families that continued. No kingdom remains whole. But in Barak Valley, pieces of each are still alive,
not in their power, but in the people who moved on without forgetting.

And that is perhaps the truest form of memory, not written in stone, but lived, unspoken, and real.

Here is the concluding part of the chapter "Kingdoms That Ruled Barak Valley", a reflective closure that ties together centuries of history, layered memory, and the unique identity of the Barak region:

Barak Valley has lived through dynasties, sultans, empires, and colonizers. But never has it belonged entirely to any of them. Each kingdom arrived with ambition, to rule, to reform, to rename and each eventually disappeared into history. What remained was not their power, but their shadow. Not their rule, but their reflection.

This valley did not resist with swords. It endured with silence. It adapted, absorbed, and folded the rulers into its language, rituals, and rhythm. Over time, it became clear, those who tried to possess Barak could not hold it. And those who walked with it quietly, left pieces of themselves behind.

Today, the people of Barak may not recite the names of kings who ruled before. But they live with the consequences, surnames passed down from Mughal sanads, rituals shaped by tribal courts, songs inherited from Sufi gatherings, and architecture with both Hindu and Persian curves. No one asks where these came from. The answer is the land itself.

To walk through Barak is to walk through a thousand quiet legacies. A prayer in a dargah echoes the past of Sufi saints who came on foot. A temple bell rings in tune with chants once heard in the forests of Kamarupa. A family name carries a forgotten appointment by a long-dead emperor. None of it is performed. All of it is lived.

That is Barak's power: it does not forget. It does not erase. And it does not break. Kingdoms may rise and fall. But the valley keeps speaking, not through monuments, but through people.

This chapter is not just a record of who ruled. It is a tribute to what remains.
And in Barak, what remains is always more than what was taken.

Notable Contributions Influenced & Region Under Control of Kingdoms

- 4th–12th Century: Kamarupa Kingdom (Varman, Mlechchha, Pala dynasties) - Entire Northeast including parts of Barak Early governance, temple architecture, Sanskrit influence
- 12th–14th Century: Gour/Gauda Kingdom (Bengal-based) - Karimganj, Southern Barak, Hindu rule, Bengal cultural influence
- 14th–15th Century: Tripura Kingdom (Manikya dynasty) - Hailakandi, Karimganj hills Extended royal control, trade, border administration
- 14th–17th Century: Bengal Sultans & Afghan rulers - Karimganj, Sylhet (overlapping) Spread of Islam, arrival of Sufi saints
    - 17th Century: Mughal Empire (Aurangzeb era, Faujdars) - Karimganj, Silchar outskirts Revenue administration, land grants (Chowdhury titles)

- Early 1800s: Dimasa Kachari Kingdom (Gobinda Chandra) - Cachar, Khaspur (Silchar) Last indigenous royal rule in Barak
- 1830s–1947: British Colonial Rule - Whole of Barak Valley, Tea estates, railways, district boundaries, Partition impact
- Post-1947: Indian Republic (Assam State) - Barak Valley Political realignment, language movement, democratic decentralization

The Pura-Pratapgarh Lineage: A Forgotten Native Dynasty of Barak Valley

I. Pura Rajya: The Origin of a Royal Legacy

In the region known today as Bundashil (Deorail), near modern-day Badarpur, once thrived a small yet culturally rich kingdom known as Pura Rajya. It was ruled by Raja Pura Singha Roy Barman, a Hindu monarch of regional influence. The kingdom's fate changed dramatically in 1397 AD (27–28 November), when a noble of Persian-Turkmen descent arrived — Malik Mohammad Sultan Mirza, the grandson of the great conqueror Taimur Long (Tamerlane). His father was Giyasuddin Mohammad Jahangir Mirza.

Sultan Mirza entered Bundashil with his grandfather during their expeditions and eventually married Princess Umaboti, the only daughter of Raja Pura. Following their union, the Pura royal family embraced Islam, marking a turning point in the region's dynastic and religious history. Raja Pura assumed the name Gayasuddin, and Umaboti was renamed Daulat Sultan.

This intercultural alliance laid the foundation for a new royal bloodline, beginning with their son Saad Malik, and continuing with Mirza Malik Kamal Uddin, preserving both Persian and regional Assamese legacies.

II. Pratapgarh Rajya: The Rise of a Borderland Kingdom

The legacy of Pura evolved further when Mirza Malik Mojlish Pratap, the grandson of Sultan Mirza, founded the Pratapgarh Rajya in the mid-15th century (c. 1450 AD). This kingdom grew to encompass large parts of present-day Karimganj district, as well as adjoining areas of Tripura and Sylhet (now in Bangladesh) — nestled between the borders of Tripura and Mizoram.

After Mojlish Pratap's death in 1492, his son Mirza Mohammad Bajid Khan assumed leadership and declared himself king. However, this declaration of sovereignty caused political friction with the powerful Bengal Sultanate, then ruled by Alauddin Husain Shah. To avoid war, a negotiation was brokered by Raja Sarwar Khan, a former minister under Bahlul Lodi. It was agreed that Bajid Khan would renounce the title of "Sultan" and adopt the title Raja Bajid Khan instead.

The lineage continued with:

- Mirza Marhamoth Khan (son of Bajid Khan)
- Jamsher Khan (son of Marhamoth Khan)
- Mirza Shakir Uddin Mohammad, who played a key role in the Mughal–Pathan conflicts of the early 17th century. In 1612, he supported the Mughal Empire against the formidable Pathan commander Khwaja Usman Khan Lohani, securing a significant victory for the Mughals.

The dynasty endured into the early 18th century:

- Raja Sirajuddin Mohammad (son of Mirza Shakir)
- Mirza Majlish Amin
- Mirza Shamsher Khan, who served as the Faujdar of Sylhet in 1723.
- He had five sons, the eldest being Aftab Uddin.

The Pratapgarh Kingdom, flourishing between 1489 and the early 1700s, remains a symbol of syncretic culture, blending Persian, Turko-Mughal, and regional identities, at the frontier of northeastern India.

Barak Valley's story is not bound by royal decrees or fading empires but by the pulse of its people and the memory of its soil. It has been a meeting ground of cultures, a confluence of beliefs, and a shelter for communities who came not with swords but with seeds of belonging. Its identity was not carved in palaces or proclaimed in courts. It was shaped in the everyday rhythm of life: in rice fields where generations toiled, in temple courtyards and village mosques where faith flowed freely, in marketplaces where many tongues mingled, and in forest paths where stories walked long before scripts arrived. The valley has held within it both stillness and movement, where change came gently, not as rupture but as layer upon layer of lived experience.

Even today, Barak Valley is more than just a region on a map. It is a living memory of co-existence, a witness to centuries of migration, worship, struggle, and renewal. Its landscape carries the scent of old legends and the promise of new beginnings. It teaches us that true legacy is not made by those who tried to possess the land but by those who became part of its breath and silence. In the quiet persistence of its people, in the continuity of its languages and rituals, in the resilience of its spirit, Barak Valley reminds us that home is not a place won it is a place remembered, tended, and understood.

XVI
Ancient Trade Routes & Geostrategy

Throughout history, kingdoms have thrived not only through force but through geography. And Barak Valley, though not always recognised in grand historical narratives, was never isolated. It was a living corridor. A route of rhythm, trade, and transfer, tucked between hills and rivers, where languages collided, spices changed hands, and stories crossed from one world into another. It was never a stagnant land waiting to be claimed. Instead, it breathed with motion. It invited movement. It welcomed wanderers, invaders, preachers, and traders alike. Every kingdom that entered the region did so with this understanding. Barak was not a borderland, not a battleground of territories to be owned, but a passage, a connector, a bridge. It was a place that held power because it allowed movement. And it held meaning because its people carried more than one world within themselves.

Even before formal kingdoms charted borders or inscribed authority on palm-leaf manuscripts, the Barak River served as a crucial artery for trade and travel. Flowing westward and splitting into the Kushiyara and Surma rivers near the Karimganj border, it connected what is now Barak Valley to ancient Sylhet, Bengal, and even down to Chittagong's coastal ports. The river was a path carved by nature, but refined by human purpose. This made the region valuable not only for what it produced — rice grown in fertile plains, timber extracted from forested hills, silk reared and spun by skilled hands — but for where it led. Control over the Barak was not simply about dominion over land. It was control over direction, over the lines that connected the inland worlds of Assam and Tripura to the port towns of Bengal. Rulers who held the river held the keys to movement between the hills and the sea, between forested borderlands and populous urban centers. The Barak was the lifeblood of exchange, not just economic but cultural and spiritual as well.

The Tripura kings, long before British rule reshaped the map, understood the power of this mobility. They taxed traders moving between present-day Hailakandi and the adjoining hill districts, ensuring a steady flow of resources into their treasury. These routes, worn into the earth by generations of footsteps, were often walked by salt and cloth merchants. Alongside them travelled Sufi saints with verses in their mouths, Brahmins carrying scriptures, and royal envoys bearing gifts and sealed letters. The foothills of Jampui and Longai did not merely serve as geographical borders. They stood as lookout points and protective watchposts, vantage spots for those who knew how to read the land like a map. These hills whispered tales of those who passed through, who camped beneath their shade, and who looked out over the valley below with intentions of diplomacy or dominion.

The Dimasa kingdom, headquartered in Khaspur near what is now Silchar, took this understanding of geography further. To them, the Barak Valley was not just a strategic territory. It was home. It was the centre from which they reached outward, not through conquest alone, but through connection. From this capital, King Gobinda Chandra sent envoys to Sylhet, to Manipur, and to the hill regions beyond. The Kachari roads they used, some of which still survive today as rugged trails weaving through dense forests and remote hamlets, were once vital arteries of administration and culture. The Dimasa kings were not distant rulers issuing orders from far-off forts. They travelled these roads, met village heads, listened to disputes, collected tributes, and offered protection. Their control over the valley came not from fear but from familiarity. They knew the terrain as one knows a song, with every bend, every ford, and every shaded grove committed to memory. Their rule was deeply intertwined with the land they moved across.

The Mughals, when they extended their imperial reach into the northeast, viewed the region through a different lens. For them, it was a zone of taxation and logistics, to be accounted for in land records and revenue charts. They established tahsils and chowkis to monitor trade. River checkpoints were placed at key junctions, not only to collect duties but to assert surveillance. Mughal-appointed faujdars in nearby Sylhet and Karimganj managed this machinery, collecting levies on goods that moved both by boat and on foot. Boats carrying areca nut, mustard, and silken cloths paid their share at the river chokis. Caravans of oxen bringing salt or dried fish from Tripura were halted, measured, and taxed. Some of these duties are still remembered in the faint ink of old family sanads and in oral traditions of ancestral lands lost over unpaid shares. It was an empire of paperwork, but one rooted in the practical realities of rivers and roads.

Even under British colonial rule, the logistical identity of the region remained intact. Instead of creating new routes, the British simply layered their own systems upon the old ones. Steamer services were introduced along the Barak and Kushiyara rivers, offering merchants quicker and cheaper ways to send goods to Calcutta. What once took days by bullock cart was now achieved with ease by riverboats, changing the rhythm of commerce. The railway line that now runs through Karimganj and Badarpur was first laid not as an innovation, but as an adaptation. It followed the geography of earlier trade paths, repackaged for industrial purpose. The British named these routes, codified them, and inscribed them on official maps, but their foundation had already been laid by centuries of movement and memory. Colonial administration did not invent connectivity in the Barak

Valley. It formalised it, often erasing the indigenous logic behind the paths it now called its own.

Why did so many rulers across centuries and empires desire the Barak? It was not only for conquest, for titles, or even for natural wealth. It was because the land led somewhere. It pointed outward. It invited passage. It held within its rivers and forests a thousand directions, each one a story of exchange. Its people, shaped by centuries of crossing and conversation, knew more than one way to speak, more than one way to live. They were multilingual not because rulers demanded it, but because rivers brought all languages with them. Sylheti, Bengali, Meitei, Dimasa, Hindi, Urdu, Arabic — these tongues were not foreign to the valley. They were native to its plural rhythm. The people of Barak were merchants who could count in two scripts, priests who translated their prayers, boatmen who understood the weather, scribes who copied letters for different courts, healers who mixed herbs from hill and plain. And through them, the valley pulsed. It was never a fringe. It was always a current.

Even today, if you sit quietly by the river at night, you may still hear those echoes. The sounds may not be loud, but they linger in the air. There are voices of boatmen calling to each other across the darkness, merchants bartering under lantern light, Mughal officials issuing demands, and a Sufi saint murmuring verses that float across the water like mist. The empires have vanished. The borders have shifted. The names of places may have changed, but the routes remain. The Barak still flows, not only with water, but with memory. It moves through forests and towns with the same patience it always had. Its bends and turns still follow ancient logic, still knowing where to slow and where to rush. And along its banks, people still live who understand its past, even if they do not speak of it. They carry the knowledge in the way they farm, the words they use, the stories they pass to their children.

The Barak has outlived kingdoms and rewritten maps. It does not cling to permanence. It survives because it flows. It endures because it carries. And as long as it moves, so too will the stories of those who once travelled its length, who once built their lives on its banks, and who still, even today, look to it for direction.

XVII
The Story of Markets That Shaped a Valley

A valley is not made only of rivers and hills. It is made of exchanges, of spices, stories, and silences. And in Barak Valley, if the temples, mosques, and homes are its heart, then the bazaar is its breath. That's where people gather, not just to buy or sell, but to belong.

Ask an old man in Karimganj about where everything began, and he might not name a kingdom. He might say Santar Bazar.

Once officially named "Centre Bazaar" a colonial attempt at clarity, the people gently refused the English and chose their own name: Santar Bazar. The name came from habit, not policy. And over time, it stuck. A simple market turned into a landmark. Not because of its architecture, but because of the way it absorbed people, the boatmen from the Kushiyara, the grocers from the villages, the women selling hand-pounded rice from Ujandihi, the Bangladeshi migrants with fish wrapped in wet cloth, the Assamese hawker with plastic goods and songs.

You don't go to Santar Bazar for one thing. You go for the air, scented with turmeric, gossip, diesel, and sweat. You go to see if "Ajoy da has reopened his paan shop," These are not shops, they are timekeepers.

In Badarpur, the market was once a stopping point for trade from the hills and the river. Here, the whispers of Sufi saints still hover around the stalls, where sugar and mustard once passed hands between merchants of different faiths. Even today, someone from Ratabari might walk half a day to buy fabric from Badarpur Bazaar,not because it'scheaper, but because "their grandfather did the same."

Premtola, with its name like a song, was once a lovers' corner in Silchar, a junction for waiting, for chai, for unsaid things. Now it's busy, rushed, overgrown with billboards, but the old-timers remember. That bench outside the medicine shop? Someone proposed marriage there in 1975. That wall with faded posters? Someone once sold banned Bangladeshi records under it.

And there's Itkhola, where even the name "bricks are unloaded here" tells of trade and building. A place named after an action, not a saint or soldier. That's what Barak's bazaars do, they hold not only goods but verbs. They do things. They hold movement.

Even weekly haats in interior villages. such as Dullabcherra or Kaliganj, are stories. Cattle, cucumbers, and cassette players sold beside each other. Transactions in Sylheti, Hindi, Bishnupriya, and silence. Some people don't come to buy. They come to ask how someone's daughter is doing in Dhaka. Or to check whether a classmate from Silchar returned from Delhi. A market is not a place. It's a pulse.

Markets are also memory spaces. A young boy still sells his grandfather's pickles under the same bamboo shade. A mother tells her son, "Your uncle bought your father's wedding kurta from that corner." Someone still wraps banana leaf around betel nut, not because it's required, but because "we've always done it that way."

And just like that, the bazaar continues.

It survives floods, inflation, migration, name changes, and elections. Governments may build malls, name roads, or shut stalls. But the people return, to where the stories are still priced by weight, and trust is weighed in fistfuls of spices.

The kingdoms are gone. The rulers forgotten. But the bazaar remains. Not as resistance, but as ritual.

XVIII
If I Were the Mapmaker

(A reflective literary essay from the author's perspective)

If I were the mapmaker, I wouldn't start with borders.
I'd start with the sound of the river.

Because when you draw a line, you must first ask: who does the river sing to? Whose childhood laughter echoed down its banks? Who buried their prayers in its currents? The river does not know your lines. It only remembers footsteps. And in Barak Valley, the footsteps came from all sides, from Sylhet, from Tripura, from Manipur, from Bengal, and from dreams.

If I were the mapmaker, I wouldn't divide the land by language.
I'd listen to how people speak at home.

Sylheti spoken here is not the same as the Sylheti in Beanibazar or Moulvibazar. It is a little softer, maybe, and often filled with borrowed tenderness from Bengali, Hindi, Bishnupriya. The mother tongue here is not just one tongue, it is many tongues braided together by grandmothers who never needed a dictionary.

If I were the mapmaker, I would not label places as margins.
I'd mark them as centers of memory.

A village that doesn't appear on a tourist map may still have a mosque older than the Republic, or a tree that sheltered refugees in 1971. A bend in the road near Hailakandi may hold the spot where a poet once sat and wrote a line that changed a generation's mood. Who decides what is important? Why do some places get names in bold, and others fade?

If I were the mapmaker, I'd ask the elders where the stories sleep.
I'd ask a boatman how far he can row before the accent changes.
I'd ask a bride what markets her mother shopped from when she was a girl.
Because history doesn't only live in forts and treaties. It lives in the things we forget to record.

If I were the mapmaker, I would leave the borders open, not for politics, but for people.
Because people carry more than papers.
They carry rituals, recipes, songs, grievances, silences.

I would draw with dotted lines, not as weakness, but as respect for the movement of lives.
I would draw Barak Valley as it is lived, not as it is filed.
I would trace the lines of migration, not just in kilometers, but in questions.
Where did your grandmother come from?
Which direction do the festival drums echo louder?
What language do you dream in?

And finally, if I were the mapmaker, I would write one sentence in the margin:

"Borders are made by rulers. But belonging —
belonging is drawn by hand."

XIX
Startups From The Mist – Real Innovators of Barak Valley

Barak Valley has long carried the reputation of being quiet, geographically distant, politically overlooked, and culturally misunderstood. But in recent years, something has changed. Amidst misty hills and river-fed towns, a new wave of entrepreneurs has begun to rise not loudly, but persistently. These are not billion-dollar startups. They are initiatives rooted in the soil, the people, and the problems of the region.

Gaurav Chakraborty – Founder, Aranyak Valley
A true son of the soil, Gaurav Chakraborty grew up in Barak Valley and later founded Aranyak Valley, a rural development initiative aimed at rebranding rural Assam through eco-tourism, community farming, and responsible storytelling. His mission: to make locals feel proud of their roots, not flee from them.

"We want rural Assam to be a source of pride, not pity," says Gaurav in an interview with EastMojo.

Handloom & Craft Revivers – Various Local Entrepreneurs
From Silchar to Hailakandi, local youth have revived bamboo crafts and handloom products, selling them online through Instagram, WhatsApp, and exhibitions. Entrepreneurs like Mohan Saikia have taken traditional skills and transformed them into livelihoods, often empowering local women and elderly artisans in the process.

These aren't just businesses, they're efforts to rescue forgotten knowledge systems.

Moinul Hoque Choudhury – Visionary of Industrial Barak

While not a startup founder in the modern sense, Moinul Hoque Choudhury deserves mention for laying the institutional foundation for many of Barak's development paths. As Commerce Minister and a prominent Barak Valley leader, he helped establish:

- ✓ Silchar Medical College & Hospital (SMCH)
- ✓ Regional Engineering College (now NIT Silchar)
- ✓ Panchgram Paper Mill (HPC) (though defunct now, it was once a major industrial hub)
- ✓ Cachar Sugar Mill (now defunct, but once a cornerstone of Barak Valley's agro-industrial ambition)
- ✓ Development of Road and Rail Infrastructure: He pushed for improved connectivity in the valley, including roads and broad gauge railway discussions, which came into fruition later.

His vision helped ignite the entrepreneurial and educational imagination of the valley.

HealthyFoodz — Nutritious Snacks Startup, Silchar

Founded in Silchar, HealthyFoodz delivers premium-quality dry fruits and healthy snacks sourced globally, almonds from California, cashews from Tanzania, and Ajwa dates from Saudi Arabia, with the aim of making nutritious food easily available to the Barak Valley community .

Vision: To redefine daily snacking habits, ensuring Barak Valley consumers enjoy high-standard healthy options without breaking the bank .

Team Karimganj – Karimganj's Global-Tech Powerhouse

In a remarkable success story originating from Barak Valley, Team Karimganj Technology Solutions Pvt Ltd.

(commonly TeamK) has emerged as one of the region's most formidable tech startups. Founded in March 2019 by Hrishiraj Bhattacharjee and a small team of five including Partha Das, Nirmal Jyoti Baidya, Alok Deb, Rishav Bhattacharjee, and Monidipto Das, the company began in modest surroundings in Karimganj town .

In just a few years, TeamK has scaled to over 150 employees, drawing approximately 110 from Barak Valley alone, and has executed full-service global contracts—collaborating with tech giants in Canada, the US, UK, France, Germany, Israel, Singapore, Australia, and New Zealand . The company specializes in open-source intelligence (OSINT), data analytics, cybersecurity, web development, dark-web monitoring, full-stack and SaaS solutions .
Team Karimganj has also prioritized social impact at home, offering free exam coaching to over 2,200 local youth, helping many succeed in government recruitment as well as supplying flood relief during natural disasters. In October 2022, it was honored as "Company of the Year" in the startup category by Business Connect.

Structurally, the business was formally incorporated on November 22nd, 2022, with Hrishiraj Bhattacharjee and Arpita Roy listed as directors, its LinkedIn page shows a team size of 51–200 staff.

Why TeamK Matters?

- Local talent on a global stage: It demonstrates how Barak is not just consuming ideas, but generating expertise used worldwide.
- Community-first approach: Their educational and disaster-relief initiatives embody regional values intersecting with business success.

- Tech-enabled identity shift: TeamK's rise, in part, challenges the narrative that innovation can only come from large cities.

deFreshBox — Silchar-Based Online Grocery Startup
Founders: Nivedita Dey and Moumita Bhattacharjee

Launched in 2021 under Oikantik Solutions Pvt. Ltd., deFreshBox offers affordable daily groceries online with free or low-cost delivery—a game-changer during and after the COVID-19 pandemic in Silchar. Notably, they price products below MRP and waive delivery fees for orders above ₹250, making online shopping accessible and safe for seniors and local families .

"We wanted to mitigate risks for shoppers while keeping prices affordable," says co-founder Nivedita, highlighting their community-first approach .

Al-Baraka Nizamia Rubber Garden – Ratabari, Karimganj
Founder & Owner: Niamat Ali

Established: Circa 2005

Located in the rural heartlands of Barak Valley, Al-Baraka Nizamia Rubber Garden is a significant regional enterprise founded by Niamot Ali. Since its inception around 2005, the garden has steadily grown into a key player in the natural rubber sector. It supplies high-quality rubber across India - including major destinations like Kolkata, Silchar, and even Kerala, known as India's rubber hub. The garden stands as a testament to local entrepreneurship, sustainable agriculture, and rural employment in the Ratabari area.

Sheetal-Pati
Shitalpati is made from cane or murta plant, variously known as mostak, patipata, patibet and paitara. Murta tree grows around the reservoirs of Sylhet and other neighbouring districts of Bangladesh.

Shitalpati is made in North eastern states of India.

Shital Pati is the traditional art of making a handcrafted mat by weaving together strips of a green cane known as 'Murta'. The mat is used by people all over Bangladesh as
a sitting mat, bedspread or prayer mat. The main bearers and practitioners are weavers living mostly in the low-lying villages in the greater Sylhet region of Bangladesh, but there are also pockets of Shital Pati weavers in other areas of the country. Both men and women participate in collecting and processing Murta, with women being more involved in the weaving process. The craft is a major source of livelihood and a strong marker of identity; primarily a family-based craft, it helps to reinforce family bonding and create a harmonious social atmosphere. Mastery of the technique commands social prestige, and the practice empowers underprivileged communities, including women. The government promotes awareness of the element through local and national craft fairs, and Shital Pati communities are increasingly being organized into cooperatives to ensure the efficient safeguarding and transmission of the craft and guarantee its profitability. Safeguarding efforts involve the direct participation of the communities concerned and the practice is primarily transmitted from generation to generation within the families of craftspeople.

In Kaliganj area of Karimganj district of Assam the patikar communities also makes shital patis for bedspread and prayer mat with beautiful designs and art. Moulana Abdul Munim Choudhury - an eminent freedom fighter of India and Member of Assam Legislative Assembly of 1962 from South Karimganj Constituency, encouraged them for making Shitalpati and export it in abroad.

UNESCO has recognised the Traditional Art of Shital Pati weaving of Sylhet and included it in the Representative List of the Intangible Cultural Heritage of Humanity.

Barak Valley Layer Farming Pvt. Ltd. – Pioneering Commercial Poultry in Silchar

Established on 22 February 2017, Barak Valley Layer Farming Pvt. Ltd. stands out as one of the region's first large-scale agribusiness startups. Based in Silchar and run by directors Shyamali Rao and Raja Rao, the company specializes in commercial layer poultry farming — producing eggs and broiler chickens in a structured, regulated environment. With an authorized capital of ₹2.15 crore and a focus on modern agri-tech methods, this venture reflects how Barak Valley's traditional farming knowledge is being transformed into formal enterprise. It is a testament to the rising confidence in agriculture as a profitable and professional venture in the region.

Barak Logistics – Driving Barak's Mobility Network

A lesser-known yet vital venture, Barak Logistics operates from Narsingpur, Silchar, and plays a key role in enabling local connectivity. Founded in 2018, this registered micro-enterprise provides vehicle leasing and transportation services crucial to small and mid-sized businesses. Its low-profile yet essential function supports Barak's rural-urban flow from ferrying construction materials to servicing employee movement across Silchar, Hailakandi, and Karimganj. In a region often hindered by road and rail bottlenecks, Barak Logistics is part of the invisible engine that keeps the valley moving.

Barak Valley Betel Nut Trading – Preserving Herbal Heritage through Commerce

Owned and operated by Ashaduzzaman, this herbal and spice goods enterprise based in JB Kalain, Silchar, brings regional commodities like betel nut, black pepper, and dry red chilli into formal trade networks. With an annual turnover between ₹50 lakh to ₹1 crore, Barak Valley Betel Nut Trading represents a growing trend where local, traditional products are not just culturally relevant but commercially viable. Its participation in the ayurvedic and herbal markets opens a bridge between indigenous practices and mainstream supply chains.

Techno Traders Pvt. Ltd. – Constructing New Silchar

Located in Meherpur, Silchar, Techno Traders Pvt. Ltd. is one of Barak's notable private players in real estate and infrastructure. With a capital base of nearly ₹2.95 crore, the

company contributes to residential and commercial development in Silchar — a town experiencing slow but steady urban expansion. Real estate ventures like Techno Traders are gradually altering the skyline of Barak Valley, offering modern housing and business spaces while generating employment for engineers, architects, and local laborers.

Assam Progressive Developers Ltd. – Building the Valley's Urban Future

Another key real estate company, Assam Progressive Developers Ltd. operates from N.S. Avenue, Silchar, with a similar capital investment of ₹2.94 crore. The firm's presence points to growing investor confidence in Barak Valley's long-term infrastructure potential. As migration, education, and commerce increase, so does the demand for organized housing and civic amenities. Firms like this are preparing Silchar and adjoining towns for a future beyond municipal limitations.

Taratari App (Silchar) – Emergency Coordination by Aranyak Valley

Developed in April 2020 during the COVID-19 lockdown by Silchar-based Aranyak Valley, the Taratari app (Bengali for "Quickly") helped coordinate volunteer relief in the Barak Valley. Created in just seven days by developers Gaurav Chakraborty, Sanjit Singh, Sujoy Deb, and Arijit Goswami, the app facilitated tracking of relief packets, volunteer registration, and liaison with district administration. It was built and deployed remotely, using basic internet and smartphones, highlighting Barak Valley's agile, problem-solving spirit .

Barak Valley Institutes of Entrepreneurship (Hailakandi)

Incorporated on 3 February 2016, this NGO is a micro-enterprise based in Hailakandi engaged in computer and peripheral equipment repair and maintenance. It represents one of the first formal entrepreneurship-focused institutions in the region, offering technical servicesand community training in IT hardware — an early step toward localized tech empowerment .

Hmar Agro Organic Producer Company Ltd. – Pineapple Power from the Hills of Lakhipur

In a region better known for its linguistic struggles and cultural depth, Cachar district is now ripening into a hotspot for organic agriculture. One of the finest examples of this transformation is the rise of Hmar Agro Organic Producer Company Ltd., a farmer-led organization that has put Lakhipur's pineapples on the national and international map.

On July 3, 2025, a remarkable event took place: the Cachar District Agriculture Office flagged off a 20-tonne consignment of organic pineapples from Lakhipur to New Delhi. These fruits weren't the product of a multinational supply chain — they were grown organically by nearly 2,000 local farmers across 1,500 hectares in Rajabazar, Binnakandi, and Lakhipur.

This initiative was spearheaded by Hmar Agro Organic Producer Company Ltd., with operational and export support from Trifac Agro Pvt. Ltd. What makes it extraordinary is not just the scale, but the intent: it's about creating sustainable income for local farmers, promoting organic methods, and making Barak Valley a credible player in export-oriented agriculture.

Dr. A.R. Ahamed, the District Agriculture Officer, stated that similar consignments have already reached markets across India and even international destinations like Dubai. In fact, a second export to Dubai is already in planning — awaiting improved road connectivity to Guwahati, which temporarily slowed logistics.

The flag-off ceremony, attended by agricultural dignitaries and local stakeholders, signaled more than a shipment. It signaled a shift — from dependency to productivity, from isolation to exportation, and from marginalization to mainstream participation.

As Barak Valley continues to search for identity and economic stability, ventures like Hmar Agro show what's possible when farmers, planners, and logistical partners work together with clarity and purpose.

From the soil of Lakhipur to the shelves of New Delhi and Dubai, this is Barak Valley's pineapple revolution in motion.

NearHive: A Social Delivery Revolution From Barak Valley

NearHive aims to redefine the way delivery apps function in India—starting right from the Barak Valley.

Originally launched as a Minimum Viable Product (MVP) to test market potential, NearHive is now ready for its full-fledged production rollout. Unlike conventional delivery platforms, NearHive brands itself as "Not Just Another Delivery App." What sets it apart is its unique fusion of social media and delivery service, positioning itself as the world's first social experience delivery app.

Users can scroll through posts, like what they see, and order the items they crave. At the same time, content creators—dubbed Hive Creators—can earn rewards, goodies, offers, and credits just by uploading content and contributing to the NearHive ecosystem. The app seeks to build a vibrant, community-driven delivery experience that benefits both consumers and creators.

What truly distinguishes NearHive is its mission-oriented approach. While big delivery corporations largely ignore Tier-II and Tier-III cities in pursuit of profits, NearHive aims to bring smart, high-quality services to underserved regions. Their goal: to empower smaller towns and make "Smart India" a reality for all, not just for urban metros.

Core Team:

- Kunal Deb – Chief Executive Officer (CEO)
- Subhajit Bhattacharjee – Chief Operating Officer (COO)
- Subhrojyoti Sen – Chief Technology Officer (CTO)
- Dipankar Deb – Chief Financial Officer (CFO)
- Baaz Rana – Advisory Director
- Saurojit Karmakar – System Administrator
- Barnik Deb – Content Head
- Alok Kumar Dey – Application Developer
- Argajit Dutta – Manager
- Pratham Mazumder – Assistant Middleman Head
- Tanmoy Chakraborty – Web Developer
- Soumyadeep Ghosh – Onboarding Head
- Ashu Rajput – Video Editor

Diaspora Innovators & Content Creator

Though not rooted locally now, several content creators from Barak Valley have made their mark in language preservation, comedy, Sylheti memes, and social commentary. While formal startups may be few, the spirit of cultural entrepreneurship is clearly alive in online spaces like:

- Sylheti Memes (Instagram/Facebook pages by anonymous Karimganj/Silchar youth)
- Sylheti vloggers in the UK, UAE, and Kolkata who draw millions of views
- Sylheti Youtubers like Barak Kantha, Northeast Comedians, Kasabangla, Tipu Khan Entertainment, ERN Comedy, etc
- Sylheti food vlogger like বুন্দিয়ার LADDU @bundiyar_ladduuu

Their contribution: keeping the voice of Barak relevant for Gen-Z.

XX
Barak Valley Starter Pack (Gen Z Edition)

This starter pack won't show up on any platform.
It's born, lived, fried, and served hot in Barak Valley.
We don't need aesthetic filters, we've got real spice!

Daily Vocabulary:
"Dimag kharap oise" = universal reply to everything
"Oi oi" = greeting / insult / warning / all of the above
"Ghum nai ni" = we're not okay but also not sleeping
"Khaiya kuno kaj nai" = no we don't have as always
"Kita khobor?"
"Kita ba"
"Baash khaiso?"

Digital Identity:
WhatsApp group name: "Area 51", mostly darker than the black colour.
Insta bio: "Half Bengali, Half Lost, Fully Hungry"
Google search: "Is Sylheti a real language?"
Shared 47 reels today. Replied to none.
Social media accounts with 0 posts & private too.

Vibe Playlist:
1 old Sylheti heartbreak song
1 romantic Hindi song that hits at 1 AM
2 lo-fi beats for "study"
1 rap track to feel like a don
That one remix of Rabindra Sangeet your cousin made

Food Fuel:
Shoishyo er Elish (Hilsa Fish with Mustard Seeds)
Muri-makha with mustard oil
Jhal aloo in tiffin
Shingara that burns your tongue and heals your soul
5 kinds of cha in one day (minimum)

Psychological Facts:
Knows 3 scripts, 4 languages, and zero career certainty
Emotionally attached to trains, rains, and torn identity cards
Believes exams are a social conspiracy
Dreams of escaping Barak, until the train leaves
Everybody is in a hurry and yet no one seems to be on time

Bonus Items:
Cousin who works in Guwahati but shows up at every wedding
Rickshaw ride trauma (but make it cinematic)
Adda spot behind school
Grandparent who still narrates 1947 like it happened last week

Things You'll Only Hear If You're Truly From Here
Because we speak in punchlines, food references, and mood swings.

"Adda isn't gossip. It's intellectual bonding over tea and ten layers of overthinking."
"Every Barak kid has a cousin who's either in Silchar College or Dubai — no in-between."
"My playlist has Sylheti, Hindi, English, Punjabi, Haryanvi, Bhojpuri, and some random YouTube instrumental remix. I am culture."
"I'm fluent in three languages and still get roasted by elders for mixing them all mid-sentence."
"Barak weddings hit different. You'll cry, dance, eat seven times, and go home with a steel bowl."
"I'm not late. I'm on Barak Standard Time."

If you know, you know.

XXI
A Note from the Author: I Have Roamed, But This Is Home

In the course of my life, I have moved through many landscapes, met countless people, and seen the beauty and contradictions of my country firsthand. Each journey left behind a fragrance of experience, but no matter how far I went, the scent of home in Barak Valley always pulled me back.

In 2012, I crossed the border and explored Bangladesh, visiting its soul-filled corners the energy of capital Dhaka, the spiritual rhythm of Sylhet, the busy port life of Chittagong – the Assam-Bengal railway's headquarters in British India, the serene coastline of Cox's Bazar Sea Beach, and the green comfort of Moulvibazar, Hingazia, Habiganj, Tajpur, and Sunamganj, Comilla. These journeys were not just about visiting another land, they were about feeling the echo of a shared ancestry.

From 2014 onward, I visited Tripura nearly five or six times, driving through its greenery, quiet lanes, and cultural simplicity. I journeyed by car from Agartala up to Sunamura, approximately 55 km by road, tracing footsteps of shared histories.

In 2019, the road took me through Delhi, Ajmer (Rajasthan), Jaipur (Rajasthan), Agra (Uttar Pradesh), and Panipat (Haryana), before reaching Amritsar (Punjab) and the Wagah Border (India–Pakistan border). I passed through the spiritual gates of the Golden Temple and stood in the historic silence that lingers in Jallianwala Bagh. I remember the resonance of the walls of Sirhind (Punjab), the energy of Mohali and the planned charm of Chandigarh. I stood still in the corporate pace of Noida (Uttar Pradesh), carrying thoughts back to a different rhythm — that of home.

In 2024, I revisited Greater Noida, Aligarh (Uttar Pradesh), and Delhi. Life began to settle around an academic orbit a university in Delhi became the new base. But the more cities I added to my path, the more I found myself writing from the memory of another place.

In 2025, Eid-ul-Fitr brought me to Bulandshahr (Uttar Pradesh), where I was warmly invited by my friend Mr. Sahil, his brother Mr. Sajid bhai, and their extended family. As someone visiting from Assam, I was embraced not just as a guest but as one of their own. Surrounded by their wide circle of friends and kind-hearted neighbours, I experienced Eid in its truest spirit — full of warmth, laughter, and togetherness. Sajid bhai's family, in particular, treated me with such affection and care that it still remains etched in my heart. From the delicious food to the generous hospitality, everything reflected a bond beyond borders — one of shared humanity and unspoken brotherhood.

Eid-ul-Zuha called me again to Jama Masjid, Delhi, an experience soaked in prayer and the sound of thousands gathered under one sky. Later that year, I revisited the tranquil Sufi ambiance of Ajmer (Rajasthan), passed through the technical calm of Roorkee (Uttarakhand), explored the spiritual atmosphere of Haridwar (Uttarakhand), and sat in reflection at Deoband (Uttar Pradesh) — places where faith breathes alongside discipline, passed through Meerut, Muzaffarnagar, Kairana, city of Shamli etc.

Yet after all of this, the most heartfelt sukoon, that deep, content sigh of the soul, comes only here, in Barak Valley (Assam). It is not just a place. It is poetry stitched in the language of belonging. The trees speak in Sylheti, the rivers remember your name, and the breeze greets you like an old friend.

I have travelled. I have wandered. But I return. Always.
Because Barak is not a stop on my map.
It is the starting point of everything I carry.

XXII
A Page of Regional Proverbs or Sayings

Old Sylheti or Bengali sayings with English translations

The word 'Sillok' in the Sylheti dialect refers to a type of proverb or folk tale. It is primarily a proverb or short story prevalent in Sylhet's rural society, usually based on a specific subject or event, from which moral lessons or life experiences can be derived.

Sillok (Proverb Or Folk Tale)
"Khazna thakia Bhazna boro!" – This proverb is used when the perceived value of something is greater than its actual utility.

"Jemon kormo, temon fol" – Similar to English proverb "As you sow, so shall you reap", this highlights the concept of karma and consequences.

"Nijor chokh furiya, onner dosh dekho" – Used to criticize people who ignore their own flaws but are quick to judge others.

"Hosh koro, bero dhoro" – A short and sharp warning or call to action: Stay aware, and act quickly when needed.
"Zaat or ghoro maro laat, bhaat or ghoro dew haat"- Kick the house of pride and caste, give your hand to the house of rice.

"Aan koite kaan, siya koite barabaan" – I'm saying one thing, but it's being heard as something else. In Hindi 'keh kuch aur raha hoon, sunn kuch aur raha hai'

"Basar tele basa biraan" – Refers to a situation where one person visited your home, and you served the food items that he brought.

"Haatey bashi, mukhey rashi." – Flute in hand, verses in mouth. Means, talks sweetly, but does nothing useful all show, no action.

"Bhitor fanka, bairey shanka." – Empty inside, bangles outside. Criticizing people who are flashy outwardly but hollow inwardly.

"Mukh diya asha, kaaj diya basha." – Gives hope through words, but beats with actions. Used for people who talk nicely but behave cruelly.

"Gach nai tali, narikel chay kali." – No palm tree, but wants tender coconut. Desiring things that are not even close to being possible.

"Matha thanda, kormo chanda." – Keep your head cool, and work will shine. Encourages calmness and smart work.

"Jinish boro kamor, na hole shoromor." – The item is either too costly or embarrassing. Used when a situation leaves you with no good choice.

"Ami ailam akta, amare koy bhaat kha" – Means I just arrived, and they're telling me: 'have some rice.' It's a classic Sylheti way of expressing hospitality, warmth, and belonging, it captures the raw, unscripted love of Sylheti culture, it's a gesture of inclusion, of saying, "You're one of us."

"Tor o ase, mor o ase, aao ura uri,
Tor o nai mor o nai, jaw dura duri"

"Naste na parile,
Utan thera"

"Jar lagiya churi korlam,
Hai koy chur"

"Mair tain mamur barir gop"

"Dada re tumi ada poraitay ni?"

"Gorom bhate bhilai bhejar,
Ar hoq mato ammoq bhejar"

"Janena bismillahr guri,
Ar biya korto mullahr puri"
"Nai mamu thakia,
Kana mamu bhala"

"Baaf e guta ar gaase guta,
Maa e zee ar gaii e ghee"

"Khaslot jayena moile,
Ar ijjot jayena dhoile"

"Mon milile mela,
Na milile ekla ekla"

"Barir goruye,
Barir gaash khaye na"

"Pek dekhar aage,
Muja khulilar"

"Hutila na teh hutila na,
Ar hutila teh utila na"

"Okkil or dhon bokkil e khaye,
Ar kanjal er dhone ghora ghori baye"

"Beelo maas, unndaal o kula,
Hori Bou ey koroin jhula"

"Manshor kutum ala awaay jaway,
Ar gorur kutum ala leaaye fusaye"

"Haathir o fara fhisle,
Ar subonnir o bora dhube"

"Gele bail ase,
Ar roile dail ase"

"Aasmaan or joto tera,
Ar case or oto dhara"

Riddles 'Foi'

Riddles are called 'Foi' in the Sylheti language. It is also a significant branch of folk literature. In riddles, the experiences gained by rural people are recorded in the form of questions.

Find answers of the following:

"Dekhray joto aitra oto,
Tar adha tar pai,
Tare loiya sho purai"

"Ami gelam tare anat,
Tare pailam potoh,
Saride more, aani giya tore"

"Shubhankar er faki,
Tinsho theke tin geele,
Roilo koto baki?"

"Ikko motir tole tole,
Bikko motir saani,
Kun jagat dekia aiso gaasor aagat paani?"

"Dekho Allahr kudrat,
Latir bitre shorbot"

"Ek bhai Hagore,
Ek bhai nogore,
Ek bhai kunagam,
Tino bhai e ek naam'

"Ek kila,
Dui boin e pindila"

"Ghor or bitre ghor,
Haath baraiya dhor"

XXIII
Eminent Personalities of the Valley

The Barak Valley has long been home to distinguished individuals who played pivotal roles in the political, administrative, spiritual, and cultural life of the region. This chapter documents and honors the contributions of such eminent personalities from civil servants and Sufi scholars to judicial officers, educationists, and freedom fighters who shaped the identity and legacy of the valley.

In addition to biographical profiles, this chapter also includes detailed listings of legislative representatives from the valley who served at various points in modern political history:

- Members of the Legislative Council of Eastern Bengal and Assam (1909–1912)
- Members of the Assam Legislative Council (1913–1935)
- Members of the First Legislative Assembly (1937–1967)
- Members of the Central Legislative Council of India (1921–1946)
- Members of Parliament (1952–1971)
- Member of Parliament (Rajya Sabha 1957–1972)

Through these names and narratives, the chapter reflects the valley's deep involvement in India's freedom movement, governance, and nation-building efforts. Each individual featured here represents a thread in the rich and diverse fabric of Barak Valley's socio-political evolution.

Legislative Representation in Barak and Sylhet (1905–1913)

The Legislative Council of Eastern Bengal and Assam was established in 1905. However, in its initial formation, there was no representation from the Barak Valley and Sylhet region. This lack of inclusion persisted until 1909, when two prominent figures, Khan Bahadur Sayed Abdul Majid and Sri Babu Dulal Chandra Deb were inducted into the council, marking the beginning of political representation from the region.

In 1913, with the annulment of the partition of Bengal, the province of East Bengal was dissolved, and the Assam Legislative Council was formed under the provisions of the *Indian Councils Act of 1909*. This new legislative body comprised 25 nominated and elected members, laying the foundation for a more structured form of governance in Assam and opening new avenues for regional participation in colonial administration.

1909:

1. Khan Bahadur Sayed Abdul Majid
2. Sri Babu Dulal Chandra Deb

1913 (Post East Bengal separation):

1. Ramani Mohan Das (Karimganj)
2. Kameni Kumar Chanda (Silchar)
3. Khan Bahadur Sayed Abdul Majid (Moulvibazar)
4. Nalini Kanta Roy Dastidar

1921–23:

1. Karimganj: Moulvi Mohammad Abdul Ahad Choudhury, Ramani Mohan Das
2. Hailakandi: Hara Kishore Chakraborty
3. Silchar: Bipin Chandra Deb Laskar, Khan Saheb Rashid Ali Laskar

1923–26:

1. Karimganj: Firoze Chandra Deb, Nazmul Islam Choudhury, Abdul Matin Choudhury
2. Hailakandi: Hara Kishore Chakraborty
3. Silchar: Bipin Chandra Deb Laskar, Khan Saheb Rashid Ali Laskar

1926–29:

1. Karimganj: Khan Bahadur Mahmod Ali, Kirodhe Chandra Deb
2. Hailakandi: Hirendra Chakraborty
3. Silchar: Jatindra Deb Laskar, Arjan Ali Mazumdar

1929–35:

1. Karimganj: Kirodhe Chandra Deb, Khan Bahadur Mahmod Ali
2. Hailakandi: Hirendra Chakraborty
3. Silchar: Sonoth Kumar Das, Idris Ali Barlaskar

First Assam Legislative Assembly Election (1937)

Silchar -

1. General: Arun Kumar Chanda
2. SC Reserved: Kala Chand Roy
3. Katigorah Silchar: Namwar Ali Barbhuiya

Hailakandi -

1. General: Hirendra Chandra Chakraborty
2. Muslim: Reserved: Mozrof Ali Laskar

Karimganj -

1. Karimganj Sadar: Khan Bahadur Abdul Majid Choudhury
2. South Karimganj: Khan Bahadur Mahmod Ali
3. East Karimganj:
   SC Reserved: Boloram Sarkar
   General: Kameni Kumar Sen

4. West Karimganj-
   SC Reserved Seat: Khirud Chandra Deb
   (expired June 2, 1937)
   ↓
   Rabindranath Aditya (by-election)
   General Seat: Mobarak Ali Choudhury

Representatives of Tea Planters (Surma & Barak):

1) Baidya Nath Mukherjee
2) P. Patwari

Assam Legislative Assembly (1946)

Silchar-

1. General: Sachindra Mohan Deb, Mukobbir Ali Mazumdar
2. SC Reserved: Nibaron Chandra Laskar

3. Katigorah Silchar: Namwar Ali Barbhuiya

Karimganj -

1. Karimganj Sadar: Abdul Latif
2. South Karimganj: Mufazzil Hussain

3. East Karimganj-
   General: Kameni Kumar Sen
   SC Reserved: Ramesh Chandra Das

4. West Karimganj: Rabindranath Aditya, Idris Ali

Hailakandi-

1. General: Babu Vidyapati Singh
2. Muslim Reserved: Abdul Mutlib Mazumdar

First Election After Independence (1952)

Following India's independence and the adoption of the Constitution in 1950, the country held its first general elections in 1952. This historic event marked the beginning of democratic governance in the newly independent nation. Conducted under the framework of universal adult suffrage, the elections were held for both the Lok Sabha (House of the People) and the State Legislative Assemblies.

In Assam, as in the rest of India, these elections brought significant political change and gave people from diverse regions, an opportunity to participate in shaping the new democratic order. It was the first time many communities experienced direct electoral participation, symbolizing a shift from colonial rule to a representative democracy.

<u>First Assembly (1952)</u>

1. Silchar: Mehrab Ali Laskar
2. Sonai (Silchar): Moinul Haque Choudhury
3. Katigorah: Namwar Ali Barbhuiya
4. Sonai: Nanda Kishore Singh
5. Barkola: Roy Chand Nath
6. Hailakandi-Silchar: Hem Chandra Chakraborty
7. Katilcherra: Gouri Shankar Roy
8. Karimganj Sadar: Rarendra Mohan Das
9. Badarpur: Maulana Abdul Jalil Choudhury
10. Ratabari-Patharkandi: Baidya Nath Mukherjee
11. Ratabari SC Reserved: Ramesh Chandra Das
12. Patharkandi-Karimganj: Khan Bahadur Mahmod Ali

<u>Second Assembly (1957)</u>

1. Silchar Sadar: Jyotsana Chanda
2. East Silchar: Moynul Haque Choudhury
3. Sonai: Nanda Kishore Singh
4. Udharbond: Tojomul Ali Barlaskar
5. Lakkhipur: Ram Prasad Choubey
6. Katigorah: Hem Chandra Chakraborty
7. Badarpur: Maulana Abdul Jalil Choudhury

↓

Bimala Prasad Chaliha,CM of Assam (by-election 1958)

8. North Karimganj: Narendra Mohan Das
9. South Karimganj: Abdul Hamid Choudhury

10. Patharkandi-
    1) General: Biswa Nath Upadhyay
    2) SC Reserved: Gupesh Nomosudra

11. Hailakandi: Abdul Mutlib Mazumdar
12. Katilcherra: Gouri Shankar Roy

Third Assembly (1962)

1. Silchar East: Moynul Haque Choudhury
2. West Silchar: Nanda Kishore Singh
3. Sonai: Pulo Kishore Singh
4. Katigorah: Tarapodo Bhattacharjee
5. Udharbond: Dwarika Nath Tiwari
6. Lakkhipur: Ram Prasad Choubey

7. North Karimganj: Ratindra Nath Sen
8. Karimganj South: Abdul Munim Choudhury
9. Badarpur: Maulana Abdul Jalil Choudhury

10. Patharkandi-Ratabari-
    1) General: Baidya Nath Mukherjee
    2) SC Reserved: Ram Deb Mala

11. Hailakandi: Ram Pirit Rudra Pal
12. Katilcherra: Gouri Shankar Roy

Fourth Assembly (1967)

1. Silchar Sadar: Sachindra Mohan Deb
2. Sonai: Moynul Haque Choudhury
3. Katigorah: Abdul Quddus Nurul Hoque Laskar
4. Borkhola: Altaf Hussain Mazumdar
5. Udharbond: Jagannath Singh
6. Lakkhipur: Merachauba Singh
7. Dholai: Jatindra Mohan Barbhuiya

8. Karimganj South: Prafulla Choudhury

9. North Karimganj: Ratindra Nath Sen
10. Badarpur: Abdul Jalil Choudhury
11. Patharkandi: Motilal Ram Kanu
12. Ratabari: Biswanath Upadhyay

13. Hailakandi: Abdul Mutlib Mazumdar
14. Katilcherra: Tojomul Ali Laskar

Central Legislative Council
Representation for Barak and Surma Valleys

During the British colonial period, the region comprising present-day Barak Valley, Surma Valley, entire Meghalaya, Dima Hasao, Mizoram, and parts of present-day Bangladesh (including four districts) was represented as one constituency in the Central Legislative Council. This vast territorial jurisdiction was collectively assigned two reserved seats-one for a Muslim candidate and one for a Hindu candidate. This system of communal representation aimed to ensure a semblance of balance between major communities, although the region's socio-political diversity was far broader.

This structure remained in place until the Government of India Act 1935, after which provincial autonomy and legislative restructuring were introduced in 1937, leading to the formation of separate legislative assemblies.

<u>1921:</u>

1. Kameni Kumar Chanda
2. Abdur Rashid Choudhury

<u>1923 & 1926:</u>

1. Sheesh Chandra Dutta
2. Abdur Rashid Choudhury

<u>1929:</u>

1. Basanta Kumar Das
2. Abdur Rashid Choudhury

1934:

1. Brajendra Narayan Choudhury
2. Abdul Rashid Choudhury

- Abdul Majid Choudhury Nominated was nominated as the representative of Assam Legislative Council to Central Legislative Council of India

1944 (By-election): Dewan Abdul Basit Choudhury (Abdul Rashid Choudhury was expired)

1946:

1. Arun Kumar Chanda
2. Moiz Uddin

Members of Parliament (Post-Independence)

1952 (First General Election)

1. Karimganj: Suresh Chandra Deb
2. Cachar-Lushai Hills: Nibaron Chandra Laskar

1957 (Second General Election):

1. Silchar: Dwarika Nath Tiwari
2. Karimganj: Nihar Ranjan Laskar

1962:

1. Silchar: Jyotsana Chanda
2. Karimganj: Nihar Ranjan Laskar

1967 & 1971:

1. Silchar: Jyotsana Chanda
2. Karimganj: Nihar Ranjan Laskar

Member of Parliament (Rajya Sabha)

03/05/1957 – 02/04/1960

- Suresh Chandra Deb

03/04/1960 – 02/04/1966

- Suresh Chandra Deb

03/04/1966 – 02/04/1972

- Mohitosh Purkayastha

Influential Figures of Barak Valley:
Dr. Ronald Ross KCB KCMG FRS FRCS

(13th September, 1857–16th September, 1932)

Dr. Ross came to the region to investigate the cause of the widespread malaria outbreak in Cachar. After conducting experiments on the cause of malaria at Lubbock Hospital, he came to the conclusion that malaria is spread by female mosquitoes. His discovery of the cause of malaria opened a new path in the medical world for the diagnosis of malaria and its prevention.

For this medical discovery, Dr. Ronald Ross was awarded the famous Nobel Prize in 1923.

Inquisitive public consciousness and keen publicity increase or decrease the importance of a subject. The current Dewan group of T.E. is located in Lakshmipur administrative subdivision of Cachar, a remote area in the north-eastern part of the country.

Sitting in a little-known medical center called Labac Hospital, Cachar under the Jaysree Tea Company, about a hundred years ago, a dedicated researcher won the world-famous Nobel Prize for his enthusiastic research.

Arjan Ali Mazumder — Lawyer & Politician of Assam (1886-1976)

Arjan Ali Mazumder was born in 1886 into a respected family of Dudpatil, Silchar. His grandfather was Abdul Gani Mazumder, a prominent figure in the region. His father, Abdul Mia Mazumder, had three sons: Nasib Ali Mazumder, Arjan Ali Mazumder, and Ahmadur Rohman Mazumder. The family had a strong educational background notably, Nasib Ali Mazumder was the first Muslim graduate of Cachar and served as an Extra Assistant Commissioner (E.A.C.), earning the title Hakim Nasib Ali.

After completing his primary and secondary education, Arjan Ali Mazumder moved to Calcutta, where he earned his B.L. (Bachelor of Law) degree.

In 1924, Arjan Ali Mazumder joined the Silchar Bar Association, becoming the third Muslim B.L. holder to practice law in Silchar. Initially residing at Rahman Patty, Malugram, Silchar for the convenience of his clients, he later relocated to Water Works Road, Silchar due to communal tensions in the area. Known for his legal acumen and integrity, he quickly gained popularity among the residents of Silchar and emerged as a respected lawyer of the district.

Arjan Ali Mazumder was a prominent figure in the civic and political landscape of Assam during the early 20th century.

Mazumder gradually stepped into public affairs and political service. In 1928, he became a nominated member (presumably of the local or provincial legislative body; the sentence seems incomplete). His early involvement in politics marked the beginning of a long and influential career in Assam's sociopolitical sphere.

He served multiple terms as a member of the Silchar Municipal Board, including in 1931 and 1934, and was also appointed to the Local Board. A committed social reformer, he was the founder Secretary of Cachar Anjuman Islamia, a role he held for six years, actively contributing to community welfare. In 1927, he was elected to the Legislative Council of Assam (MLC) from the Silchar Muhammad-en seat, where he played a significant role in legislative debates and discussions.

Arjan Ali Mazumder passed away in 1976 at the age of 90. His legacy was carried forward by his son, Altaf Hussain Mazumder, an advocate of the Silchar Bar, who later served as an MLA from Borkhola and became a Minister in the Government of Assam. His two grandsons, Dilwar Hussain Mazumdar & Mehbub Hussain Mazumdar are also serving as a Lawyer at District Bar, Silchar.

Dr. Jane Helen Rowlands

(1891 - 1955)

She was a pioneering Welsh missionary, educationist, feminist, and scholar whose legacy continues to shape the cultural and academic landscape of Karimganj in Assam. She was born in 1891 in Wales, a constituent country of the United Kingdom, known for its rich traditions in nonconformist Christianity, poetic heritage, and a deep-rooted emphasis on education, equality, and social reform. Though small in size, Wales produced many passionate missionaries during the 19th and early 20th centuries, and Dr. Rowlands was among its most remarkable daughters. She arrived in India in 1916 under the Welsh Calvinistic Methodist Mission and devoted her life to education, women's empowerment, and social upliftment. Fluent in Bengali and deeply engaged with local culture, Dr. Rowlands was also an outstanding academic, earning a Doctorate in Literature from the Sorbonne in Paris for her landmark thesis La Femme Bengalie dans la Littérature du Moyen-Âge, which explored depictions of Bengali women in medieval literature. In Karimganj, she taught English,

Bengali, and Philosophy at Karimganj College, where her photograph still hangs in the principal's office and a section of the library is named "Rowlands Hall" in her memory. Her compassion extended beyond classrooms, she founded Dipti Nibash, a home for widows and orphans, and established a dispensary to provide medical relief to the underprivileged. One of her most enduring legacies is the Rowlands Memorial High School on Church Road in Karimganj, which remains a respected institution especially for girls' education. Dr. Rowlands passed away in Karimganj in 1955 and was laid to rest there, remembered as the last European missionary buried in the region. Her life exemplified the spirit of Wales and the United Kingdom, a commitment to service, learning, and humanity that transcended borders.

Arun Kumar Chanda - Founder Principal A.K. Chand Law College

A.K. Chanda Law College derives its name and inspiration from Arun Kumar Chanda, a distinguished freedom fighter, social reformer, and visionary leader of Assam. Born on 17 February 1899 in Silchar, Arun Kumar Chanda dedicated his life to the cause of national independence and social justice. He actively participated in the Indian freedom movement, mobilizing people in the Barak Valley region against colonial oppression. Besides his political activism, he was also a renowned social worker and writer who edited the Bengali weekly Saptak, using it as a medium to spread awareness about nationalism and social reforms. His life reflected the ideals of courage, sacrifice, and service to society. Unfortunately, Arun Kumar Chanda passed away on 25 April 1947, a few months before India achieved independence.

The establishment of A.K. Chanda Law College in his honor was a recognition of his contribution to the socio-political awakening of Assam. Although Arun Kumar

Chanda himself was not a legal academic, his name and legacy as a reformer became the guiding spirit for this premier institution of legal education in Barak Valley.

A.K. Chanda Law College was founded in the year 1960 in Silchar, Cachar district of Assam, with the aim of imparting quality legal education and promoting justice in society. It is one of the oldest law colleges in the region and has played a significant role in nurturing competent legal professionals over the decades. The college is affiliated with Assam University, Silchar and its academic programs are approved by the Bar Council of India (BCI), ensuring that its graduates are eligible to practice law throughout India.

From its inception, the college has emphasized both theoretical and practical aspects of legal education. It offers a three-year LL.B. degree program under the semester system. In addition to classroom teaching, A.K. Chanda Law College actively organizes moot court competitions, legal aid clinics, and guest lectures by legal experts to enhance students' professional skills. Its Legal Aid Cell provides free legal services to the marginalized sections of society, reflecting the institution's commitment to social responsibility and justice.

Over the years, the college has produced several eminent advocates, academicians, and judicial officers who have contributed to the legal system of the country. Under the present leadership of Dr. Abu Taher Talukdar, the college continues to uphold its legacy of excellence while adapting to contemporary legal challenges.

Khan Bahadur Abdul Majid Choudhury

Khan Bahadur Abdul Majid Choudhury was a highly respected political and social leader from Karimganj, in the Barak Valley region of Assam, during the late British colonial period. He held the distinguished title of "Khan Bahadur", a recognition awarded by the British Raj to Indian citizens for their meritorious public service and community leadership. Abdul Majid Choudhury was widely admired for his commitment to education, civic welfare, and the upliftment of the Muslim community in pre-independence Assam.

He served as a Member of the Assam Legislative Assembly from the Karimganj (Central) Muhammadan constituency during the 1937–1946 term, a period of great political transformation under the Government of India Act, 1935. As a legislator, he actively represented the interests of the people of Karimganj and Sylhet region, working toward the development of education, rural infrastructure, and communal harmony. His leadership was instrumental in navigating the challenges of colonial governance, growing demands for Indian self-rule, and regional identity assertion in the culturally rich Sylhet–Karimganj belt.

Beyond his political achievements, Khan Bahadur Abdul Majid Choudhury was a devout and principled man, known for his generosity and wisdom. He earned the honorific "Hazi" after performing the pilgrimage to Mecca, which further elevated his stature in society. He hailed from a prominent and educated Muslim zamindar family in the Karimganj area, rooted in a legacy of social leadership and public service.

One of his most distinguished legacies is his son, Advocate Abdul Muqtadir Choudhury, who followed in his father's footsteps in public life and went on to become a Minister of Assam. Abdul Muqtadir Choudhury played a vital role in post-independence Assam politics and legal affairs, continuing the family tradition of leadership, education, and public service. The legacy of Khan Bahadur Abdul Majid Choudhury lives on through the contributions of his descendants and the enduring respect he commands in Karimganj's history.

Mukabbir Ali Mazumder - Renowned Politician, Lawyer & Freedom Movement Participant
(1901-1965)
Mukabbir Ali Mazumder was born in 1901 in Ambikapur, Silchar. He began his early education at Ambikapur Maktab and later completed his Matriculation from Silchar Government High School in 1919, securing a First Division. He pursued higher education at M.C. College, Sylhet, earning a L.A. degree, and subsequently graduated with a B.A. and B.L. (Law) from Dhaka University, Bengal.

After completing his law degree, he joined the Silchar Bar in 1933 and quickly established himself as a respected and reliable lawyer. For the convenience of his legal practice, he shifted residence from Ambikapur to the heart of Silchar town. Mukabbir Ali Mazumder was known not only for his legal expertise but also for his dedication to the causes of justice and public welfare. He served as GovernmentAdvocate for the Department of Forest, Assam, for many years and became the General Secretary of the Silchar Bar Association in 1952.

He left behind two sons Nurul Alam Mazumder, who became a prominent advocate and politician & he was the Chairman of the Advisory Board of Bishkut Dargah Sharif Development Soceity, Karimganj and Fakhrul Alim Mazumder, who served as Vice Chairman of the Athai Committee of Silchar Municipality. Nurul Alam Mazumder also served as Chairman of the Silchar Development Authority in 1985.
Mukabbir Ali Mazumder began his political journey during his student life at M.C. College, Sylhet, becoming actively involved in the Khilafat and Non-Cooperation Movement launched in 1919 under the leadership of

Mahatma Gandhi, Maulana Azad, and the Ali Brothers. He gave up his studies temporarily to organize meetings and rallies in support of the movement.

Initially a member of the Indian National Congress, he was also part of the Bengal Provincial Congress Committee. However, with the rise of communal politics and the growing influence of the All India Muslim League, he left Congress in 1938 and joined the League. He rose to the position of General Secretary of the District Muslim League in 1944.

He entered local governance as a Member of the Silchar Municipality in 1942, and soon after, was appointed Vice-Chairman of the Silchar Municipal Board. In 1946, he was elected as a Member of the Assam Legislative Assembly (MLA) from the Silchar Reserved Constituency as a Muslim League nominee.

After India's independence and partition, he returned to the Indian National Congress in 1949. He also served as Chairman of the Silchar Local Board from 1946 to 1950 and was a Member of the Cachar Minority Cell in 1950.

Mukabbir Ali Mazumder played an active role in the Language Movement of Barak the leaflet titled "Apapracharer Pratibad", dated 25 July 1961, which strongly protested against defamatory publications targeting Maulana Abdul Jalil Choudhury, a respected Islamic scholar and leader.

Dr. Triguna Kumar Sen

(24 Dec 1905 - 11 Jan 1998)

He was a distinguished Indian freedom fighter, educator, academic leader, and statesman whose life's work significantly shaped modern India's educational and political landscape.

He was born in the village of Birosri, Karimganj (then part of British India), and his ancestral home was in

Maizgram, Karimganj. He began his early education at 1 No. Mohanganj Lower Primary School in Sadarashi, Karimganj. From these humble beginnings, he rose to become one of India's foremost educationists and policy-makers.

Key Achievements:

- Dr. Triguna Sen actively participated in India's freedom movement during British rule, contributing to the struggle for independence through both activism and intellectual engagement.
- First Vice-Chancellor of Jadavpur University (1956–1966): He helped build the institution from the ground up, nurturing it into a hub for progressive technical and liberal education. His student-friendly, democratic leadership style is still remembered fondly.
- 11th Vice-Chancellor of Banaras Hindu University (1966–1967): Tasked with restoring order during a phase of intense student agitation, he succeeded by establishing direct trust and communication with students.
- Union Minister of Education (1967–1969): Under Prime Minister Indira Gandhi's government, Dr. Sen led the creation of the National Education Policy of 1968, aimed at universalising and modernising education in India.
- Union Minister of Petroleum, Mines and Metals (1969): As a cabinet minister, he introduced significant regulatory measures like the Drug Prices Control Order, shaping India's health and industrial policies.
- Member of Parliament, Rajya Sabha (1967–1974): Representing Tripura, he continued to serve the nation by shaping policy and legislation in the upper house of Parliament.
- Padma Bhushan Awardee (1965): Dr. Sen was honoured with the Padma Bhushan, India's third-

highest civilian award, for his extraordinary contributions to education and public service.

Legacy:

- Institutions like the Triguna Sen Auditorium at Jadavpur University.
- The Triguna Sen School of Technology in Assam continue to uphold his vision.
- His role as a freedom fighter, nation-builder, and educational pioneer remains a source of inspiration across generations.

Dr. Sunawar Ali Chowdhury

Dr. Sunawar Ali Chowdhury was born at Hamindpur, Sutarkandi, Karimganj. He completed his Master's Degree and earned a Ph.D from Calcutta University, where he was awarded a Gold Medal for his academic excellence. Following his studies, he joined the Indian Railway Service. Later, became associated with the Eastern Bengal Railway, which, after the Partition of India, became Bangladesh Railways. He retired as the General Manager of Bangladesh Railways. Now his descendants reside in Dhaka.

Monwar Ali Chowdhury

Monwar Ali Chowdhury was born at Hamindpur, Sutarkandi, Karimganj, graduated in Engineering from Calcutta and joined the railway service. After independence, he moved to Chittagong, where the headquarters of the then Assam Bengal Railway was located. It is necessary to mention here- In 1947, at the time of partition of India, the Bengal Assam Railway was divided into two parts. The 2,603,92 km of track located in East Pakistan, came under the control of the central Government of Pakistan. On 1st February 1961, the Eastern Bengal Railway was renamed the Pakistan Eastern Railway was transferred to the Government of East Pakistan.

After holding various key position with the Indian Railway and Bangladesh Railway, he eventually retired as Divisional Tele-Communication Engineer and settled permanently at the port city Chittagong. Now his descendants live in USA. Note that, he was the son-in-law of Dr. Rosman Ali Choudhury, renowned Zamindar family of Ujandihi, Karimganj.

Jitendra Kumar Choudhury - The Founder Principal of Gurucharan College

Gurucharan College, popularly known as G.C. College, was established on 15th July 1935 in Silchar, Assam, and stands as one of the oldest and most esteemed institutions of higher education in the Barak Valley. The college was founded through the generous endowment of Gurucharan Paul, a noted tea planter and philanthropist, whose vision was to promote higher education in a region that lacked adequate academic infrastructure at the time.

The college began its journey under the pioneering leadership of Jitendra Kumar Choudhury, who served as the Founder Principal. A dedicated educationist and visionary, Choudhury played a crucial role in shaping the academic and administrative framework of the institution in its formative years. With a small team of faculty and limited resources, he laid the foundation for a culture of academic rigor, discipline, and community service that would define G.C. College for decades to come.

Initially affiliated with Calcutta University, the college started with intermediate and undergraduate courses in Arts, later expanding to include Science and Commerce streams. With time, it became affiliated with Gauhati University, and eventually with Assam University, Silchar, after its establishment in 1994.

Over the decades, Gurucharan College has grown into a premier center of learning in Northeast India, producing generations of scholars, professionals, educators, and public servants. The institution continues to thrive, upholding the ideals envisioned by its founder Gurucharan Paul and carried forward by Jitendra Kumar Choudhury, whose legacy remains etched in the college's enduring pursuit of excellence in education.

Prof. P.C. Bhattacharjee - The Founder Principal of Karimganj College

Prof. Prafulla Chandra Bhattacharjee, widely known as P.C. Bhattacharjee, was a pioneering educationist and the Founder Principal of Karimganj College, established on 1st August 1946. At a time when access to higher education was limited in the Barak Valley region, Prof. Bhattacharjee emerged as a guiding force in shaping the academic landscape of Karimganj and its surrounding areas. A man of scholarly depth and administrative vision, he laid the institutional foundations of the college with dedication and foresight. Under his leadership, Karimganj College began its journey with modest resources but a strong commitment to academic excellence. Prof. Bhattacharjee worked tirelessly to build an environment conducive to learning, fostering a culture of discipline, inquiry, and integrity among students and faculty alike. His contribution not only ensured the successful establishment of the college but also set high standards for future academic growth. Remembered as a humble yet determined leader, his legacy continues to inspire generations of students and educators in southern Assam.

Sri Ranendra Mohan Das

Son of Ramani Mohan Das. He was a distinguished political leader and social worker from Assam who played a significant role in shaping the socio-political landscape of the Barak Valley during the post-independence period. A respected figure in public life, he dedicated his career to the service of the people, particularly focusing on the welfare and development of Karimganj district.

Ranendra Mohan Das rose to prominence as a legislator when he was elected to the Assam Legislative Assembly in the 1957 general elections, representing the Karimganj North constituency. His election to the Assembly marked an important milestone for the region, as he worked diligently to address local issues such as rural infrastructure, education, and agricultural development.

Apart from his political achievements, Sri Das was deeply committed to social causes. He advocated for better educational facilities and worked to improve access to schools in remote areas, believing education to be the foundation of progress. His leadership reflected integrity, foresight, and a strong sense of responsibility toward the common people of Assam.

His contributions during the 1950s and 1960s remain etched in Assam's political history. Today, he is remembered as a leader who combined political acumen with social service, leaving behind a legacy that continues to inspire the region.

Sri Ranendra Mohan Das served as the Chairman of the Assam Public Service Commission (APSC) during the period 1975–1976. He holds the distinction of being the only person from the Barak Valley to have ever held the post of APSC Chairman.

Rathindra Nath Sen

Sen was a prominent political figure from Karimganj district, Assam, remembered for his tenure as a legislator during the early decades of Assam's post-independence politics. He served as an Independent Member of the Assam Legislative Assembly from the

Karimganj North constituency, securing consecutive victories in the 1962 and 1967 assembly elections. At a time when party politics had not yet firmly consolidated its grip in the Barak Valley, leaders like Sen commanded respect and popularity based on their personal reputation, grassroots work, and strong connection with the people.

The political atmosphere of Karimganj in the 1960s was quite dynamic. The region was still adapting to its new realities after the Partition of 1947, which had left Karimganj as part of India, while Sylhet was merged into East Pakistan (now Bangladesh). Leaders such as Rathindra Nath Sen emerged as voices of stability and development during this transitional period. His victories as an independent candidate, defeating the major parties of the time, signified the trust placed in him by the electorate who valued local leadership over party affiliations.

As a representative of Karimganj North, Sen focused on addressing the everyday challenges faced by the people of the district. The Barak Valley was grappling with issues like flood management, connectivity, agricultural support, and trade, especially as Karimganj shared an international border with East Pakistan. Sen's tenure was marked by efforts to bring government attention to these matters, and he remained closely engaged with his constituents, which strengthened his image as a people's leader.

By the early 1970s, the dominance of national parties such as the Indian National Congress began to reshape the political landscape in Karimganj. In the 1972 elections, Rathindra Nath Sen was succeeded by Abdul Muqtadir Choudhury (INC), marking the end of the independent leadership era in the constituency. However, Rathindra Nath Sen's contributions during the formative years of Karimganj's political journey remain significant, as he was among the leaders who helped the region transition into a stable democratic framework while safeguarding its unique cultural and economic identity.

Mahbubur Rab Choudhury

(January 1915 – January 1997)

He was a prominent freedom fighter, social reformer, educationist, and local leader from present-day Karimganj district in the Barak Valley of Assam. He was born in Dholchara (now renamed Choudhury Tilla) under Patharkandi police station, in what was then Cachar district. He was the son of Gulam Mazhar Choudhury and Malikun Nesa Choudhury, and a descendant of Mirza Malik Mohammad Turani as well as Sultan Bayazid Khan (Sultan Bazid) of the historic Pratapgarh principality. He belonged to the only zamindar (Choudhury) family of the village.

Choudhury began his education at Dakshinbagh Prabhlabhi School, Maulavibazar, and later joined Sylhet Government School. However, he refused admission there when asked to sign a circular barring students from political activities, choosing instead to study at Sylhet Pyarimohan Public Academy, where he completed his schooling. He pursued higher studies at Islamia College, Calcutta, but his participation in anti-British movements prevented him from appearing for examinations. He later joined M.C. College, Sylhet, completing his Intermediate of Arts in 1939 and graduating with a B.A. in 1941.

His political journey began as a student in 1931 when he co-founded the Surma Valley Student Federation with peers such as Raman Sushikar Das, Aravind Kar, and Sailendra Kumar Choudhury. He was also associated with the Nikhil Bharat Students' Federation and played an active role in the Krishak Sabha movement. For his involvement in anti-colonial activities, he was imprisoned multiple times, including during the

All India Jallianwalabagh Day protests in 1939, 1940, and 1941.

After India's independence, Mahbubur Rab Choudhury devoted himself to community service and education. He served as President of the Village Panchayat, President of the Regional Panchayat, Chairman of the Karimganj Sub-Divisional Council, and Chairman of the School Board. He established educational institutions, including Jafargarh M.E. School at Baraigram and L.P./M.E. Dhalchera at Ichaganj, and was an advisor to the Karimganj Freedom Fighters' Welfare Association. He also actively supported the Barak Valley language movement, advocating for the cultural and linguistic rights of the Bengali-speaking population.

In the 1970s, he contested the Patharkandi Assembly constituency election as an independent candidate, where he emerged as the runner-up. For his remarkable contributions to India's freedom struggle, the Government of India awarded him the Tamrapatra (Copper Plaque) in 1972 on the Silver Jubilee of Independence. His name remains etched in the history of Karimganj as a fearless leader who harmonized education, social reform, and nationalist ideals.

Hazrat Shah Sufi Shafeequl Islam Choudhury

Choudhury was an eminent personality and a deeply pious individual, son of Amin Ali Choudhury, Zamindar of Bishkut, Karimganj. He served as the Sheristadar of the District Judge Court, Sylhet, a prestigious administrative post in the Indian judicial system. A Sheristadar was the chief administrative officer of the court, responsible for receiving and examining court pleas. The term originates from the Persian word sarishta-dār, meaning "Administrative Officer of the Court".

A brilliant student from a young age, he received his early education at the Government High School of Karimganj Town, later graduating from M.C. College, Sylhet.

In his early years, he was a distinguished educator at the historical Bishkut Dargah Sharif Madrassa, an institution founded by the revered Islamic scholar and Sufi saint of the Indian subcontinent, Hazrat Shah Sufi Abdullah Bhadeshwari (R:).

He later served in the District Judge Court, Cachar, before joining the District Judge Court, Sylhet, where his dedication and integrity elevated him to the high-ranking position of Sheristadar.

Beyond his official duties, he was devoted to spreading Islamic knowledge.

He personally taught the Holy Qur'an to numerous high-ranking officials in the Sylhet district headquarters, leaving a lasting spiritual impact on many.

Through his perseverance and tireless efforts, he attained excellence both in his profession and spiritual life. He was honored with the Caliphate of Allama Hafezzi Huzur (R:) and continued to serve the cause of Islam with unwavering dedication until his passing.

He has two sons and four daughters. His sons, Hafiz Maulana Mufeezul Islam Choudhury and Hafiz Muheeul Islam Choudhury, continue to uphold his legacy.

Shishir Ranjan Kar Shastri - The Founder Principal of S.S. College, Hailakandi

Srikishan Sarda College (S.S. College), Hailakandi, was established on 18th September 1950, and stands as one of the most respected and enduring institutions of higher education in southern Assam. The college was named in honour of Sri Srikishan Sarda, son of Sri Srichand Sarda, a prominent tea planter and philanthropist whose family generously contributed to the establishment of the institution. The foundation of the college was made possible through the combined efforts of many local well-wishers, with special mention to Late Pratap Chandra Nath, who donated the land on which the college stands.

At the heart of this historic foundation was Shishir Ranjan Kar Shastri, who served as the Founder Principal of S.S. College. A renowned scholar, educationist, and community leader, Shastri was entrusted with the responsibility of leading this new institution during a time when Hailakandi lacked advanced educational infrastructure. Under his visionary leadership and tireless efforts, the college started functioning with Higher Secondary and Degree courses in the Arts stream. His strong academic values, administrative efficiency, and close bond with the local population ensured that the institution took root and grew with stability and prestige.

In 1958, the college expanded to introduce the Science stream, and later added the Commerce stream in 2013–14, reflecting its dynamic and inclusive approach to education. Over the years, S.S. College became affiliated with Gauhati University, and later with Assam University, Silchar, after its establishment in 1994. It is recognized under UGC Acts 2(f) and 12(B), and was accredited with a Grade A (CGPA 3.12) by NAAC in 2011-the first such distinction in the region.

Shastri's leadership laid a strong foundation not only in academic terms but also in shaping the moral and intellectual environment of the college. His influence can still be felt in the institution's commitment to empowering first-generation learners from rural, agricultural, and economically challenged backgrounds. Today, S.S. College boasts state-of-the-art facilities, career-oriented courses, a vibrant academic culture, and national-level research collaborations, all of which stand as a testament to the vision and dedication of Shishir Ranjan Kar Shastri.

Rashida Haque Choudhury - First Muslim Woman Minister from Northeast India at the Union Level

Rashida Haque Choudhury (née Majumdar), born on 24 April 1926 in Tezpur, Assam, holds the distinction of being the first Muslim woman from Northeast India to serve as a Union Minister. She was appointed Minister of State for Social Welfare, with additional responsibilities for Education and Culture, in the Charan Singh government from 1979 to 1980.

Her ancestral roots trace back to the village of Hatirhar in Cachar district, Assam, a region known for its cultural richness and historical significance.

Belonging to the respected Majumdar family, she was the daughter of Alhaj Nasib Ali Majumdar, a district magistrate and a respected figure in society. Her formative years were shaped by this intellectual and service-oriented background, which inspired her to pursue public life. She was married to Moinul Hoque Choudhury, a towering political figure in Assam and a former Union Minister himself. Their partnership represented a remarkable union of two influential leaders from Barak Valley, both committed to public service and national development.

Educated at Lady Brabourne College, Kolkata, Rashida joined the Indian National Congress in 1950 and was later elected to the 6th Lok Sabha from the Silchar constituency in 1977. Her induction into the Union Cabinet during Prime Minister Charan Singh's tenure marked a historic moment-not only for Muslim women but for the political representation of Northeast India as a whole.

A firm advocate of education and social reform, Rashida Haque Choudhury left behind a legacy of dedication, grace, and pioneering leadership. Her name remains etched in the political and social fabric of Assam and India.

Dr. Lutfur Rahman

Dr. Rahman was a prominent political figure from Assam who served as the Cabinet Minister for Public Works Department (Roads & Buildings) in the Sarat Chandra Sinha-led ministry from 1972 to 1978. Representing the Barkhola constituency, Dr.Rahman played a significant role in the development of infrastructure in Assam during a formative period in the state's post-independence history. His tenure was marked by efforts to improve road connectivity and public infrastructure, particularly in the Barak Valley region. A respected leader within the Indian National Congress, Dr. Rahman emerged as a key representative of the minority community in the political landscape of Assam. His contributions to the region's development and his role in state politics during the 1970s earned him recognition as one of the influential ministers of that era. Though detailed biographical records are limited, his legacy continues to be remembered in the political history of the Barak Valley.

Carrying forward his legacy of service, Dr. Rahman's children have made significant contributions in diverse fields. His son, Dr. Mohammad Masoom, is a well-known paediatrician based in Silchar, Assam. Renowned for his dedication to child healthcare and his compassionate approach to medicine, Dr. Masoom has earned the trust of countless families across the region.
Among his daughters, Dr. Kismat Sultana serves as the Head of the Department of History at Karimganj College. A scholar with an M.A. and Ph.D., she holds

the position of Associate Professor and is respected for her academic contributions to the field of history.

Another daughter, Mrs. Asmat Sultana, is an Professor at Rabindra Sadan Girls' College in Karimganj. Associated with the Arts faculty, she continues to play a role in nurturing academic growth among young women in the region. She was united in marriage with Engineer Nasir Uddin Mazumder, a highly respected Superientendent Engineer of PWD. Following years of dedicated service, he retired with honour, leaving behind a legacy of integrity and excellence.

Advocate Shawkat Sultana, another daughter of Dr. Rahman, is a practicing lawyer affiliated with the Silchar District Bar. Her work in the legal field reflects the family's broader engagement with public service and justice.

Together, the children of Dr. Lutfur Rahman continue to uphold the values of education, service, and leadership that defined his life and political career.

A. F. Golam Osmani (Abul Fazal Golam Osmani)

- Born: 1 April 1933, Cachar District, Assam
- Father: Late Wazid Ali Barbhuiya (also known as Golam Wazid Barbhuiya)
- Passed away on 31 March 2009 at AIIMS, New Delhi, succumbing to lung cancer

Education:

- B.A., LL.B.; Barrister-at-Law from Lincoln's Inn, London

Professional Background:

- Practiced law in Silchar from the early 1960s
- Former Principal, A. K. Chand Law College, Silchar

Political Career:

- Served as Cabinet Minister (1978–1981) handling PWD, Supply, Irrigation & Power, Veterinary, Animal Husbandry & Fishery
- Founder President, United Minorities Front (UMF), Assam – 1985
- Co-founded UMF in 1985 in response to the Assam Agitation, representing non-Assamese speaking minorities

Member, Assam Legislative Assembly:

- Elected in 1978 from Barkhola constituency, Cachar district.
- In 1985, elected MLA from Jania constituency under UMF of Barpeta.

Member of Parliament (Lok Sabha): Barpeta constituency:

- 12th Lok Sabha (1998–2003)
- 14th Lok Sabha (2003–2009)

Party Affiliations:

- Janata Party (1970s)
- United Minorities Front (formed 1985; later merged with Congress before 1998 polls)
- Indian National Congress (from late 1990s until passing)
- Other Roles & Contributions:
- Editor of the Silchar-based cultural/political journal Barak
- Active in socio-cultural causes: Secretary of the Tagore Society for Cultural Integration, member of NGO Satadal Sahayak Samiti, and Secretary of Silchar Bar Association in 1976.

Advocate Mahbubur Rahman — Founder Principal, Karimganj Law College

Advocate Mahbubur Rahman was a renowned legal luminary of the Karimganj District Bar. He earned distinction not only as a skilled advocate but also as a visionary educationist and philanthropist. He was the founder and first Principal of Karimganj Law College, a pioneering institution that contributed significantly to legal education in the Barak Valley. A respected scholar, he was widely admired for his contributions to both law and society.

He was the father of three sons and one daughter. His youngest son, Mr. Jafar Mohammad Azizul Karim Tapadar, currently serves as Civil Judge (Senior Division). His son-in-law, Advocate Sirajul Haque, is an eminent Public Prosecutor and a former Professor at Karimganj Law College.

His legacy continues through his grandsons Mr. Jewel Mohammad Zakaria, LL.M., and Junnoon Mohammad Zulfikar, B.A. LL.B. (Hons).

Advocate Mahbubur Rahman's younger brother, Advocate Abdur Rashid, is also a reputed lawyer in the district. In addition, three of his nephews are actively practicing law, upholding the family's long-standing association with the legal profession.

Abdul Muqtadir Choudhury

Son of Khan Bahadur Abdul Majid Choudhury, born on 2nd August 1938. He completed his Master's Degree and LL.B. from Calcutta University,

Abdul Muqtadir Choudhury was a prominent political leader from Karimganj district of Assam, known for his multiple tenures as a Member of the Assam Legislative Assembly. Representing the Indian National Congress (INC), he played a key role in shaping the political dynamics of the Barak Valley during the late 20th century. He was first elected as an MLA from Karimganj North constituency in 1972, which marked the beginning of his political prominence. Later, he shifted to the Karimganj South constituency, winning successive elections in 1978, 1983, 1985, and again in 1996, making him one of the longest-serving Congress leaders from the region.

As a legislator, Abdul Muqtadir Choudhury was known for his strong grassroots presence and his efforts to address the socio-economic concerns of Karimganj, a district with a unique cultural and linguistic identity within Assam. His tenure coincided with the politically turbulent period of the Assam Agitation (1979–1985) and the signing of the Assam Accord, during which leaders from Barak Valley had to balance the interests of their constituents with the broader state politics. Choudhury's repeated victories reflected his ability to command the trust of the people, particularly in a constituency that was both ethnically diverse and politically significant.

He contributed to raising issues of infrastructure, connectivity, and educational development in Karimganj during assembly sessions. As an elected representative, he sought to highlight the region's challenges, including flood control, tea garden workers' welfare, and the development of road and rail links with the rest of Assam and neighboring states. His association with the Congress party also gave him an important role in state-level decision-making during the governments led by the party in Assam.

Abdul Muqtadir Choudhury's political career left a lasting impact on Karimganj's representation in the Assam Assembly. Though the later years of his career saw increased competition from regional and independent candidates, his influence as a seasoned politician of the Barak Valley remained significant. His repeated electoral victories demonstrated his popularity and his ability to connect with the people of Karimganj across different decades. Note that, he was the son-in-law of Dr. Rosman Ali Choudhury, renowned Zamindar family of Ujandihi, Karimganj.

Abdul Noor Choudhury

Noor Choudhury was an eminent and influential personality of the greater Katigorah area. A successful businessman and Mohaldar of the forest, he was actively associated with various non-governmental organizations and also served as a Social Judge.

Owing to his extraordinary personality and foresight, people respected and willingly abided by his verdicts. He played a key role in the development of several educational institutions in the locality and was known for his numerous philanthropic initiatives. Even today, he is fondly remembered by the people with deep respect.

Md. Hussain Ahmed Choudhury — Economist & Senior Government Officer, Assam

Son of Moulana Abdul Bari Choudhury, Md. Hussain Ahmed Choudhury was born in October 1942. He began his schooling at Srigouri High School and continued his academic journey at Karimganj College, where he completed both his Pre-University and B.A. (Hons.) in Economics. He later obtained his Master's degree in Economics from Gauhati University. Though he enrolled in LL.B. at Shillong Law College and successfully cleared the Intermediate Law Examination, he could not complete the full course.

Md. Choudhury joined the Department of Economics and Statistics, Government of Assam, as a Research Officer. Over the course of a sdistinguished career in public service, he held several key posts:

- Deputy Director (1985-1991) - Posted in Dhubri
- District Joint Director (1991-1998) - Served in Karbi Anglong and North Cachar Districts
- Additional Director (1998-1999) - Until his demise

He was known for his dedication, sincerity, and commitment to public service. Md. Hussain Ahmed Choudhury passed away on 9th July 1999, just 16 months before his scheduled retirement, leaving behind a legacy of integrity and service to the state of Assam.

Mamazzad Ahmed Choudhury alias Babu Choudhury

Choudhury is an educator, researcher, poet, social worker and writer. He is the descendant of Nawab Jan Muhammad Khan Bahadur, Faujdar of Bihar & the then Srihatta, great-grand son of Zamindar Dewan Arman Ali Choudhury, the landlord of Ujandihi, grand son of Dr. Munshi Rosman Ali Choudhury and son of Nazir Ahmed Choudhury.

He was honoured with the Chishti title by *Shah Syed Abdul Ghani Gurdezi*, *Khas & Chief Khadim of Ajmer Dargah Sharif*, through the Head Office Ziarat-e-Khwaja, Ajmer Sharif, Rajasthan.

Serves as the Executive Trustee of the Bishkut Dargah Preservation and Development Trust, Secretary (Mutawalli) of Karnamadhu-Bishkut Idgah Committee, Karimganj. Secretary of Bishkut Dargah Madrassa and Nizamia Educational Research Centre and involved with various non-governmental organisitions.

Debattama Saha — From Television to Rising Bollywood Actress

Debattama Saha is an Indian actress and trained classical singer who has earned a loyal fanbase through her natural acting, expressive eyes, and elegant presence on screen. Born on 20th March 1997 in Silchar, Assam, she grew up in a culturally rich household. Her father, Ujjal Saha, worked as a senior section engineer with the Northeast Frontier Railway, and her mother, Maitreyee Saha, supported her early interest in the arts, especially classical dance and Rabindra Sangeet. Debattama completed her schooling at Don Bosco High School in Silchar and later graduated in English Honours from Amity University, Kolkata. She also has a younger sister named Ojaswita.

Debattama's acting journey began with Bengali television. She debuted in the serial E Amar Gurudakshina on Colors Bangla, where she played multiple roles: Soi, Uma, and Nayantara. Her background in classical dance added authenticity to her character and quickly made her stand out. Her transition to Hindi television came in 2019 when she was cast as Dr. Parineeti "Pari" Ganguly in Sony TV's Ishaaron Ishaaron Mein. Her portrayal of a spirited and independent doctor opposite Mudit Nayar resonated with audiences, and interestingly, she even choreographed the show's promotional dance.

Her major breakthrough came in 2020 when she was cast in the lead role of Anokhi Bhalla in Shaurya Aur Anokhi Ki Kahani on StarPlus. The show tackled themes like gender equality, women's education, and empowerment, and Debattama's character was central to its progressive message. Her chemistry with co-star Karanvir Sharma, who played Shaurya, became immensely popular and the two were fondly called #ShaKhi by fans. The serial ran successfully and firmly established her as a leading name in Hindi television.

In 2022, Debattama took on the title role in Zee TV's Mithai, the Hindi remake of a popular Bengali serial. To prepare for her role as Mithai Gosain, a sweet-seller from Mathura, she learned the Braj Bhasha dialect. This dedication to her craft reflected her growth and commitment as an actress. In 2024, she appeared as Krishna Joshi in Colors TV's show Krishna Mohini, once again playing a strong, central character.

While primarily known for her television work, Debattama also explored other creative formats. She featured in several Hindi music videos, many of which gained millions of views on YouTube. Her performances in tracks like Jo Tera Howega, Aankhein Band Karke, and Mubarak Ho were well received. She not only acted but also lent her voice in songs like Ranjhana, composed by Vikram Montrose. Her singing ability and emotional depth in such projects showcased her versatility beyond acting.

In 2023, Debattama made her Bollywood debut in the film Shehzada, where she played Nisha Upadhyay, the sister of Kartik Aaryan's character. While it was a supporting role, it marked her entry into commercial Hindi cinema and broadened her presence beyond television. The film, directed by Rohit Dhawan, gave her a platform to be seen by a much wider audience.

Debattama Saha's journey from Silchar to Mumbai reflects the story of a small-town girl with big dreams, who turned her love for the performing arts into a thriving career. Balancing television, music, and now film, she remains one of the most promising and beloved young actresses in India today. Her story inspires many from the Barak Valley and beyond to pursue their passion with discipline, humility, and heart.

Notable Civil Servants and Magistrates:

- Anfar Raja Choudhury, ICS — Secretary, Calcutta City Municipal Corporation:
  Anfar Raja Choudhury was a prominent Indian Civil Service officer hailing from Hatkhola, Pratapgarh, Karimganj. He served as the Secretary of the Calcutta City Municipal Corporation, playing a key role in urban administration during British rule.

- Mahmadur Rahman Choudhury, ICS — Indian Civil Service Officer:

Son of Moshrof Ali Choudhury of Malua, Karimganj, Mahmadur Rahman Choudhury was an officer of the prestigious Indian Civil Service (ICS). His service included several important administrative roles in colonial India.

- Mohi Uddin Choudhury, ICS — Central Excise Commissioner, East Pakistan:
  Mohi Uddin Choudhury, son of Ghose Uddin Choudhury of Umarpur village, Badarpur, Karimganj, served as the Central Excise Commissioner of East Pakistan. He retired in 1957 and passed away in 1958. His distinguished career marked him as one of the highest-ranking officials from the region during the transitional period after Indian independence and partition.

- Ahmadur Rahman Choudhury — Judicial Magistrate,Karimganj:
  Ahmadur Rahman Choudhury held the post of Judicial Magistrate at Karimganj, contributing to the administration of justice in the district during the late colonial or early post-colonial period.
- Babu Surendra Nath Sen — Judicial Magistrate (circa 1940):
  Babu Surendra Nath Sen, son of Sambhu Nath Sen, served as a Judicial Magistrate around 1940. He was among the early Bengali Hindu magistrates in Karimganj, playing a judicial role during a period of significant legal and political transformation.

- Mohammad Muzaffar Ali Choudhury — Judicial Magistrate, Sylhet (d. 1873):
  The son of Mohammad Monior Choudhury, a zamindar, Mohammad Muzaffar Ali Choudhury served as a Judicial Magistrate at Sylhet. He

died in 1873 while still in government service. His residence was at Rahatpur, Masly, Bhanga Bazar, Karimganj.

- Mohammad Shatir Ali Choudhury — Magistrate, Chapghat Pargona (1893–1912):
Son of Mohammad Jabir Choudhury, Mohammad Shatir Ali Choudhury served as the Chapghat Pargona Magistrate from 1893 to 1912. He resided in Rahatpur, Masly, Bhanga Bazar, Karimganj, and was known for his fair and long-standing judicial service in the rural pargona system.

- Jafar Md. Azizul Karim Tapadar — AJS, Civil Judge (Senior Division), Golaghat:
Son of Advocate Mahbubur Rahman, the founder Principal of Karimganj Law College, Jafar Md. Azizul Karim Tapadar was born on February 2, 1983. He was selected in the Jawahar Navodaya Vidyalaya entrance test in 1993 and joined JNV, RK Nagar in 1994. He completed his Class X under CBSE in 1998 and passed his Higher Secondary in 2000 from the same school. He then pursued a B.Sc. with Honours in Botany from Karimganj College (2000-2003), followed by an M.Sc. in Botany from Cotton College, Guwahati (2003-2005).

  Later, he pursued LL.B. from Karimganj Law College between 2005 and 2008. In 2012, he was selected for the Assam Judicial Service and is currently serving as Civil Judge (Senior Division) at Golaghat, Assam.

Prominent Authors & Historians of Barak Valley

Cachar District:

- Prof. Topodhir Bhattacharjee – Retired Vice-Chancellor, Assam University, Silchar; renowned literary critic and cultural historian.
- Abid Raja Mazumdar – Retired Principal, Nehru College, Lakhipur.
- Sanjib Deb Laskar – Retired Principal, Borkhola Higher Secondary School.
- Sabbir Ahmed Choudhury – Faculty, MCD College, Sonai.
- Prof. Habibullah Mazumdar – Department of History, Assam University, Silchar.
- Advocate Emad Uddin Bulbul – Historian and writer, Katigorah.
- Abdul Sukkur Barbhuiya – Historian and social writer, Baskandi.
- Kazi Motahir Ali – Teacher, Siddheshwar HS School, Katigorah.
- Pradeep Dutta Roy – Journalist, writer, and activist, Silchar.
- Prof. Subir Kar – Faculty, Assam University, Silchar.
- Sanat Kumar Koiri – Researcher and writer, Hospital Road, Silchar.

Hailakandi District:

- Ali Haidar Laskar – Retired Principal, SS College, Hailakandi.
- Prof. Abul Hussain Saberi – Faculty, Lala Rural College.
- Vijay Kumar Dhar – Retired Principal, SS College, Hailakandi.
- Gojeng Singh Malakar – Retired Teacher, Lala HS School.
- Mashuk Ahmed Mazumdar – Independent scholar and chronicler from Kanchanpur.

- Allama Taybur Rahman Barbhuiya – Islamic scholar and retired Principal, Hailakandi Senior Madrassa.
- Gouri Purkayastha – Author, Purkayastha Bari, Hailakandi.

Karimganj District:

- Nishit Ranjan Das – Retired Principal, NC College, Badarpur.
- Kamal Uddin Ahmed – Retired Principal, Karimganj College.
- Prof. Sujit Choudhury – Retired Principal, RS College, Karimganj.
- Banlbrata Roy – Historian and author, Ramani Road, Karimganj.
- Prof. Shib Tapan Bashu – Faculty, NC College, Badarpur.
- Jonmojit Roy – Noted for works combining literature and historical narration, Steamerghat Road, Karimganj.
- Maulana Azizul Hoque – Teacher, Jam-e-uloom Nizamia Title Madrassa, Ratabari; expert in Islamic education and cultural documentation.
- Kamruzzaman Choudhury – Cultural writer and chronicler of Bhanga, Karimganj.
- Achitcharan Choudhury – Chronicler of Moina, Patharkandi region.
- Badruzzaman Choudhury – Writer from Malua, Karimganj.
- Vivekananda Mohanta – Cultural contributor, Vidyarthi-1, Settlement Road, Karimganj.
- Shamlal Das – Historian of Anandapur, Sonbeel, Karimganj.
- Mohammad Tahir – Philosopher from Singharia, Nilambazar, Karimganj.
- Ranjit Choudhury – From Chittoranjan Lane, Karimganj.

Prominet Sufis of The Valley:

Hazrat Shah Sufi Adam Khaki (R:)

Hazrat Shah Adam Khaki (R:), was a distinguished Sufi saint and spiritual reformer of the Indian subcontinent. He is remembered for his piety, simplicity, and tireless efforts in spreading the message of Islam through love and spiritual wisdom.

Shah Adam Khaki (R:) hailed from a deeply spiritual lineage that had long been devoted to Islamic scholarship and the propagation of faith. Born into a family known for piety, he was nurtured in an environment where Qur'anic education, Hadith, and Sufi spiritual training were central. From a young age, he exhibited a profound inclination toward spiritual learning and detachment from worldly pleasures.

He sought knowledge under eminent scholars and Sufi masters of his time. His title "Khaki[10]"reflects his unmatched humility and spiritual depth. After years of rigorous training, he was bestowed with Khilafat[11] by his mentor, granting him the responsibility to guide seekers of truth.

Renowned for his deep meditation and ascetic lifestyle, Hazrat Shah Adam Khaki (R:) attracted disciples from various parts of the region. He was known for his ability to inspire people through compassion and spiritual magnetism rather than mere preaching.

Hazrat Shah Adam Khaki (R:) dedicated his life to spreading the message of Islam peacefully. He traveled extensively, settling in various places where he established centers of learning (khanqahs) and mosques. His efforts contributed significantly to the spread of Islam and spiritual awakening among the local population, particularly in Bengal and Assam.

---

[10] humble as dust

[11] spiritual succession or spiritual caliphate

He emphasized the values of love, humility, service to humanity, and submission to Allah. His approach was inclusive and harmonious, which endeared him to people across different faiths.

Numerous accounts speak of his spiritual blessings (karamat). He was said to have performed miracles that reaffirmed people's faith in God. However, he remained deeply humble, always attributing these to Allah's will rather than personal ability.

Hazrat Shah Adam Khaki (R:) passed away in a state of spiritual fulfillment, leaving behind a vibrant legacy of disciples and khanqahs. His dargah (shrine) is located at Badarpur, Karimganj, which became a center for spiritual seekers and devotees who continue to visit to this day, seeking blessings and inspiration from his life.

His teachings still resonate, emphasizing that true closeness to Allah lies in humility, selflessness, and service to creation. The descendants and followers of Hazrat Shah Adam Khaki (R:) continue to preserve his mission and teachings across the Barak Valley and surrounding regions.

Hazrat Syed Shah Abdul Karim Mujarrad[12] (R:) – The Namesake of Karimganj

Shah Abdul Karim (R:) was among the spiritual companions of Hazrat Shah Jalal (R:), arriving in Sylhet around 1303 CE. In 1308 CE, he settled along the Kushiyara River at present-day Roynagar, near Hadargram Jam-e-Masjid. Known for his simplicity, discipline in faith, and deep spiritual aura, Shah Abdul Karim inspired the local population to embrace Islam through his conduct rather than force or persuasion.

---

[12] The title "Mujarrad" means "celibate"-a mark of his lifelong dedication to spiritual life, having never married or pursued worldly pleasures.

A marketplace organically developed near his khanqah, which came to be known locally as Karim Shah'r Bazar. Over time, the settlement was named Karimganj in his honour. He was laid to rest in front of the Hadargram mosque, where his shrine[13] remains a site of spiritual reverence.

Sikandar Ghazi – Gorkapon, Badarpur

Sikandar Ghazi, another of the 360 Auliyas came in 1306 CE at Badarpur, played a dual role as a spiritual teacher and administrator of Sylhet. He chose to reside in Gorkapon, Badarpur, on the banks of the Barak River. Today, a small mosque stands at the spot where he once lived, and in front of it, embedded in the sand, is a mid-sized iron bangle, believed by locals to be associated with him. His contributions to local administration and spirituality continue to be remembered with quiet reverence.

Shah Badaruddin – The Namesake of Badarpur

Shah Badaruddin, a Sufi preacher known for his missionary zeal, arrived at what is now Badarpur in 1306 CE and lived in a fortified area made of mud, later taken over by the Mughals. He served as a commander and a religious figure, living among soldiers and preaching the message of Islam. In remembrance of his presence and contributions, the locality was named Badarpur, meaning "settlement of Badar."

Hazrat Piar Moulavi Saheb

The shrine of Hazrat Piar Moulavi Saheb (Piar Molik), revered as Piar Moulavi Saheber Mukam, is located in the southern part of Bishkut village in the Karimganj district of Assam.

---

[13] mazar

According to local tradition, Hazrat Piar Moulavi Saheb once worked as a cowboy for a villager in Bishkut. He was given a separate room to stay in. One night, the house owner's wife entered his room and was astonished to see it filled with light despite the absence of any lamp. She immediately informed her husband, who, realizing that the saint possessed supernatural spiritual powers, released him from his duties. They subsequently allotted him a plot of land on a nearby hillock.

Following this, the descendants of Habibur Raza Choudhury, who hailed from the lineage of Nawab Jan Muhammad Khan Bahadur, granted Hazrat Piar Moulavi Saheb a large tract of land. On this land, a massive pond was excavated, and a beautifully decorated mosque was built. However, historical accounts narrate that King Gour Govinda of Srihatta later dispatched his army, which demolished the mosque using elephants.

Hazrat Piar Moulavi Saheb is remembered as one of the 360 Awliya (saints) who accompanied Hazrat Shahjalal Mujarrad-e-Yemeni (R:) during his spiritual mission in the Indian subcontinent.

Syed Khwaja Amber Shah – Chishti Sufi of Bosla Bazar

Syed Khwaja Amber Shah, nephew of Khwaja Moinuddin Chishti of Ajmer, carried the Chishti Sufi spirit to the Barak Valley, came in 1306 CE at Bosla, South Badarpur. He was known for publicly offering the azaan in what is now Bosla Bazar, where his presence left a spiritual impact on the local population. After his death, he was buried at Lamarkhola Eidgah, where his shrine still receives visitors seeking peace and blessings.

Shah Sufi Baksh Ali Iraqi

Baksh Ali was a distinguished Sunni alim from Iraq, believed to have arrived in Delhi around 1315-1320 AD during the peak of the Delhi Sultanate. As a young seeker of knowledge, he devoted himself to the spiritual tutelage of the renowned saint, Hazrat Khwaja Syed Nizamuddin Auliya (R:), residing for several years at his khanqah. After the completion of his religious education and training in the Sufi path, he was directed by Hazrat Nizamuddin himself to journey eastward and spread the light of knowledge and spirituality. Following this divine instruction, Shah Baksh Ali undertook a long journey by horse and reached the eastern frontiers of Bengal, ultimately arriving in the present-day Karimganj district of Assam. Near the Ratabari Police Station, at a serene location now known as Kochukhawri, he established a mosque that remarkably still stands today-a silent witness to centuries of devotion and community learning.

There, Shah Baksh Ali Iraqi became a towering spiritual figure of the region, imparting not only Islamic teachings but also broader knowledge and wisdom to people of all walks of life. His legacy as a revered Sufi mystic is preserved in numerous local tales and mystical anecdotes that continue to echo in oral traditions. Among his descendants emerged another eminent Sufi-Musabbir Ali-a wandering mystic known for his spiritual presence and travels on horseback. Like his forefather, Musabbir Ali too became the subject of many folk legends, adding further to the mystique of the Iraqi lineage that brought divine light to the lush frontiers of eastern India.

Gohar Khan – The King of Badakshan

Gohar Khan, a Moghul prince of Badakhshan, a historic region nestled between present-day Afghanistan, Iran, and Central Asia. Gohar Khan, recognized in historical sources as the Moghul Khan of

Kashgar, succeeded Sulayman Shah in 1519 AD as the ruler of the Yasin region, an area that held strategic and cultural significance on the frontiers of the Mughal world. Their dynasty was part of a broader Central Asian tradition where governance, trade, and Sufism often intertwined.

His ancestral homeland, Badakhshan, was famed for being the world's only known ancient source of lapis lazuli, making it a vital node in early trade networks. Historically part of Tukharistan, the region extended from Balkh to the Pamir Mountains, and its people, mainly Tajiks and Pamiri language speakers, carried a rich legacy of Islamic mysticism, scholarship, and resilience.

Gohar Khan, a respected forefather whose legacy continued through his son, Nawab Ali Choudhury. From Nawab Ali Choudhury came Najib Ali Choudhury, whose name carried the family's honour into the next generation. His son, Abdul Ahmed Hye Choudhury and Ghulam Rab Choudhury, upheld the family's dignity and values, which were passed down to his own son, Abdul Munim Choudhury. From Abdul Munim Choudhury came a daughter of grace and wisdom, Jakia Aktar Choudhury - the beloved grandmother of the author.

From the handwritten papers of Hafiz Qari Maulana Ahmed Abdul Hye (R:), the eldest son of the Muhajir-e-Makki Maulana Najib Ali Choudhury (R:), it is known that Hazrat Maulana is a descendant of King Gauhar Khan (R:) of Badakhshan In Afghanistan. King Gauhar Khan (R:) gave the kingdom to his younger brother in 1056 AH 1646 AD and took the ancestral Quran Majeed written by Mir Hussain and decorated with the gold of Mohammad Yusuf (R:) and reached Delhi during the reign of the Mughal dynasty with the aim of propagating and spreading Islam. On the orders of the Sultan, he settled in the village Bagbari of Karimganj police station in Srihatta district, which is now part of Karimganj district of Assam state.

Muhajir-e-Makki Maulana Najib Ali Choudhury (R:) was a 19th-century Indian Islamic scholar and Alem-e-Deen. He was notable for establishing the first madrassa, Madinatul Uloom Bagbari, in southern Assam and the greater Sylhet region.

He was the caliph of Imdadullah Muhajir-e-Makki, a Sufi scholar of the Chishtia order. He is known to have fought against the British in Shamli, Uttar Pradesh, as an associate of Muharjir-e-Makki Imdadullah (R:), a part of the Greater Indian Rebellion against the British in 1857. After the failure of the rebellion, both men left the Indian subcontinent and migrated to Mecca Sharif. After staying there for a long time, they returned to the land of Hindustan as per the unseen instructions of the Prophet Muhammad ﷺ. In 1873, the late Najib Ali Chowdhury returned to his native village and established an Islamic higher educational institution named 'Madinatul Uloom Bagbari Najibiya Alia Madrassa' in his own house. This Madrassa is the oldest Islamic higher educational institution in North East India, which later gained great fame and reputation in the subcontinent and gifted thousands of Ulama to the community.

This educational institution is considered to be the first madrassa in the greater Sylhet region, providing a quality religious education unlike the existing informal institutions there. It played a very important role in producing scholars of the Arabic language in the greater Sylhet region, a reputation it has maintained to the present day.

Maulana Najib Ali Choudhury (R:) achieved considerable fame and reputation, and various accounts of his spiritual powers are known in folklore. After his death, his grave was converted into a shrine through the efforts of his students, which is currently located in Rautgram, Karimganj district.

Maulana Ghulam Rab Choudhury, an independent Islamic scholar and grandfather of Maulana Abdul Munim Choudhury, former member of the legislative assembly of Karimganj South. Maulana Golam Rob Choudhury (R:) the son of late Najib Ali Choudhury (R:) was one of the caliphs of Hazrat Allama Mashoud Bishkuti (R:).

Ten generations later, Gohar Khan's lineage continued to make its mark in India. One of his descendants, Abdul Munim Choudhury, emerged as a freedom fighter, a leader of the Indian National Congress, and the MLA of South Karimganj South in 1962. He was the father of the author's grandmother, Jakia Aktar Choudhury, thus connecting a centuries long legacy of spiritual guidance and public service.

An important archaeological artifact, a stone Arabic epigraph dated 1509, is preserved at the Bagbari Jam-e-Masjid. The inscription commemorates the construction of a mosque in Surjyadas village by Sher Malik, an officer of Sultan Alauddin Husain Shah of Bengal.

Fig: The epigraph was brought to Bagbari by Moulana Abdul Munim Choudhury, a descendant of Najib Ali Choudhury, respected freedom fighter, and former MLA. This artifact stands as a testament to the region's deep historical and Islamic heritage.

Fig: Posthumous honors to freedom fighter, prominent social worker, former MLA Hazrat Maulana Abdul Munim Choudhury, by Emarat-e-Shariah & Nadwatut Tameer Initiative.

Shitalong Shah (Maulana Salimullah) (1794 - 8 Dec' 1889)

Born in 1794 in Hilchar, Srigouri, Chapghat, Karimganj. Shitalong Shah, son of Jaha Baksh Ali, was no ordinary soul. He studied at the Fulbari Madrassa of Sylhet and later at the Ajiria Madrasa under the guidance of Shah Abdul Wahhab Choudhury-an institution that blossomed into a hub of Sylheti Nagri literature.

A Sufi mystic, a poet, and a master of the Sylheti Nagri script, he is remembered for his deeply symbolic and mysterious stories-tales speak of him roaming forests atop a Royal Bengal tiger. His verses echoed devotion, simplicity, and spiritual depth, passed on in handwritten Nagri manuscripts that still survive in the valley's collective memory.

He passed away on 8 December 1889 in Barotaukri, Chapghat (Zakiganj, now in Bangladesh), near the sacred confluence of the Barak, Kushiyara, and Surma rivers. In his honour, a mosque and madrassa bear his name-standing not just as structures of brick, but as monuments of mysticism and legacy.

Written By Shitalong Shah:

"শাহ আব্দুল আলি মোর পীর দস্তগীর
হাসিল মুরাদ অলি বাতিনে জাহির।
মুর্শিদ কামিল মোর শাহ আব্দুল ওহাব
তিনি প্রসাদে হৈল ধিয়ানেতে লাভ"।
অন্য জায়গায় তিনি বলেছেন-
"দ্বিতীয় মুশিদ মোর শাহ আব্দুল কাদির
শিশুকালে কেরামতি আছয়ে জাহির।"
অন্যত্র ও তিনি লিখেছেন-
"এই দুই সাহেব পীর মুর্শিদ কামিল
কৃপায়ে রব্বানী এতে মুরাদ হাসিল।"
আরেক জায়গায় ও তিনি উল্লেখ করেন-
"এই দুই ছাহেবে মোরে রাখিয়া কৃপায়
ভেদ মর্ম শিক্ষা দিলে ও ওজু নিখায়।"

"শিতালং নাম মোর গুনাহ বেসুমার
কৃপা যদি কর আল্লা করিম গফ্ফার।
মোহাম্মদ উল্লাহ দোষগুণে মাজুর
জাঁহা বক্শ আলি নাম পিতার মাশুর।
পরগণে চাপঘাট মোর পয়দিশ সেথায়
শ্রীগৌরী মৌজায়েতে, হিলচর কিত্তায়।

Allama Abdullah Bhadeshwari Bishkuti (R:)

Allama Abdullah Bhadeshwari (R:) was a towering Islamic scholar, Sufi scholar, Triple M.A., Bengali–Persian poet, and globally respected debater, born in Bhadeshwar, Sylhet. His father, Muhammad Azim Choudhury, was a well-known zamindar of Bhadeshwar and a respected figure in the region.

His ancestor, Hazrat Shah Champa Baghdadi (R:), was a soldier and peer[14] of Hazrat Shah Jalal Mujarrad-e-Yemeni (R:). He accompanied Shah Jalal from

[14] spiritual disciple

Baghdad, the capital of Iraq, to Sylhet in 1303 AD during the historic conquest of Sylhet.

He began his early Islamic education at Fulbari Alia Madrassa, Sylhet, and later matriculated from Calcutta. He graduated from Presidency College, Calcutta, and completed his postgraduation (M.A.) from Calcutta University. He continued his pursuit of religious learning at Calcutta Alia Madrassa, followed by Rampur Title Madrassa, where he earned a postgraduate degree in Arabic literature. Later, he studied Persian language and literature and completed another postgraduate degree from Peshawar.

He was a fluent and eloquent poet in both Persian and Bengali, and became widely admired for his intellectual debates and scholarly contributions. His knowledge spanned the secular and the spiritual, East and West.

After completing his studies at Calcutta Alia Madrassa, he met the world-famous Sufi scholar Shams-ul-Ulama Mufti Golam Salmani (R:), who became his murshid[15]. Upon his murshid's instructions, Abdullah Bhadeshwari (R:) traveled to Rampur and Peshawar for further studies. After returning to his master, he received 'Ilm-e-Ma'rifat[16] within six months and was granted the status of Pir-e-Tariqat[17].

Thereafter, following his murshid's command, he embarked on a 12-year journey on foot, accompanied by his khadim Shah Abdul Latif of Moulvibazar, to perform ziyarat[18] of 1300 prophets across various countries. After visiting Karbala, he traveled to Masjid Al-Aqsa, and through miraculous means, reached the suburban areas of Madinah.

---

[15] spiritual mentor

[16] Divine spiritual knowledge

[17] spiritual guide

[18] Pilgrimage

That very night, the Mutawalli of Masjid-an-Nabawi, Syed Abbas Al-Hussaini (R:), received a dream from the Prophet Muhammad ﷺ, who said:
"Abdullah Bhadeshwari is my guest, along with his khadim. Bring them to the guesthouse and treat them as my honored guests."

The next morning, Abbas Al-Hussaini (R:) sent four camels and four men to bring them. He hosted them with utmost hospitality and narrated the dream. He then unlocked the gates of the Prophet's sacred chamber, as the key custodian of the Roza Mubarak, and allowed Abdullah Bhadeshwari (R:) to enter and perform ziarat inside the blessed chamber of Prophet Muhammad ﷺ. He also visited the sites of various Sahaba (companions of the Prophet), and performed Hajj that same year.

Upon returning to India, Zamindar Dewan Muhammad Chadir Choudhury of Ujandihi and Zamindar Muhammad Azam Ali Choudhury of Bishkut welcomed him and donated a large amount of land and residential house. He settled in Bishkut, Karimganj, permanently where he devoted himself to waz mahfils[19], seminars, and preaching across the Indian subcontinent. His words were revered, and his teachings reached countless seekers of knowledge and truth. He passed away on 1918.

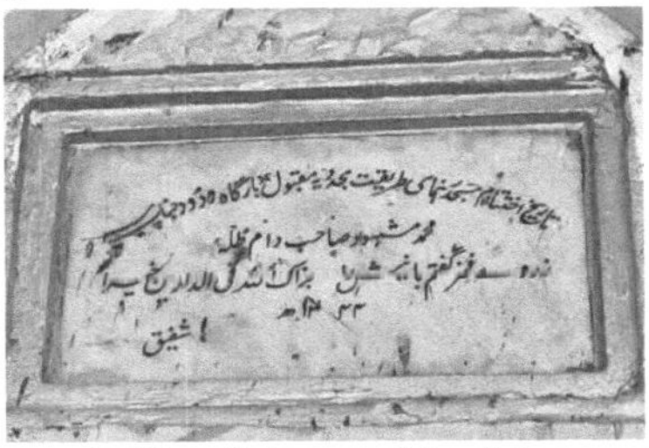

Fig: Bishkut Dargah Sharif Jam-e-Masjid, construction of the masjid was started by Allama Abdullah Bhadeshwari (R:) and completed by his son Mashoud Bishkuti (R:), on 1344 Hijri/1925.

---

[19] Spiritual gatherings

Hazrat Shah Mashoud Bishkuti (R:), the son of Abdullah Bhadeshwari (R:), Engineer turned Sufi & scholar of Tasawwuf, received his early Islamic education at home. He completed matriculation from Karimganj Government School, and obtained I.Sc. Then persuaded marine engineering in London. He was later appointed as an engineer in a French shipping company.

However, during the departure of the last Hajj of Abdullah Bhadeshwari (R:), his son Mashoud came to bid him farewell and offered money for the journey. His father declined thrice, and finally dropped the money into the water from the ship's window symbolizing disapproval of his worldly occupation. Realizing this, Mashoud sent a telegraph resignation and returned home.

After returning from Hajj, Abdullah Bhadeshwari met his son at the residence and he was then sent to Mujaddid-e-Zaman Hazrat Abu Bakkar Siddique Al-Qureshi (R:) of Furfura Sharif, Hooghly. There, he studied Islamic sciences and Ilm-e-Tasawwuf for three years and received Khilafat. Upon returning to Bishkut, he also received khilafat from his father. After the death of Allama Bhadeshwari, he took over the charges and guided the disciple, ran madrassa, orphanage, khaneka-sharif. Later, he passed away on 28th May 1949 (14 Jaishtha 1356 Bangla).

Allama Nizamuddin Bishkuti (R:), elder son of Shah Mashoud Bishkuti (R:), was born on 14th August 1927. In 1943, he secured first position in matriculation across Assam. He graduated with honors from Cotton College in 1948, and completed his Islamic education at Calcutta Alia Madrassa in 1951.

He was a fearless freedom fighter and contributed a lot to the freedom movement of India. At that time, he joined active politics. Inspired by the warm blood of youth and the love of the country of respected Walid Sahob[20], he jumped for the freedom of the country and to free the nation from the chains of subjugation. His dream was one and unique India. He could never accept the division of India. In 1947, he formed a movement against the partition. Finally, he gave up his mind and took charge of the management of the Khanka Sharif Musafir Khana and Langar Khana of Bishkut Darbar. He also contributed a lot to communal harmony. He had good relations with people from all walks of life, regardless of race, religion and caste. He was well acquainted with the national leaders of the then India. After India's first Prime Minister Pandit Jawaharlal Nehru arrived in Karimganj, he met him at the Karimganj Circuit House and took strong steps to maintain communal harmony.

Fig: Bishkut Dargah Sharif Guest House, foundation stone laid by Allama Nizamuddin Bishkuti (R:)

A deeply spiritual and active figure, he performed Hajj 47 times, visited 147 countries, and became a global Islamic scholar of Tasawwuf. In 1964, through a miraculous event, he relocated to Hingazia, in Sylhet district of East Pakistan (now Bangladesh). There, he established multiple educational institutions, madrassas, masjids, orphanages, and cultural centers across Bangladesh, India, the UK, and the USA.

---

[20] Father

The great saint whose spiritual biography was one of the highest-ranked in this realm of Tasawwuf. His heart was radiant with divine love for Allah and His beloved Prophet ﷺ. This noble soul, whose name shines in the world of Ma'rifah, was known as Shah Sufi Hazrat Maulana Muhammad Nizam Uddin Choudhury (R:), widely revered as Allama Bishkuti (R:) across the globe. People believed that reflecting upon the life and teachings of Hazrat Allama Bishkuti (R:) will inspire a new awakening in their personal, social, and national lives, helping to purify them of stagnation, immorality, and injustice, and motivating them to wage inner spiritual struggle (rectification of human nature). Hazrat Allama Bishkuti (R:) was one such illuminated being. Despite enduring immense personal trials, he remained steadfast.

Thousands of people from different faiths embraced Islam through his call and began following the way of the Prophet ﷺ in pursuit of Allah's pleasure. Even in his old age, ignoring physical hardship, he continued to spread the divine light from door to door. Hazrat Allama Bishkuti (R:) was a master and guide of multiple spiritual orders including Qadiriyya, Chishtiyya, Naqshbandiyya, Mujaddidiyya, Muhammadiyya, and Waisiyya traditions.

He passed away on 23rd March 2009, and his shrine (mazar) is located adjacent to Shahi Masjid, Hingazia, Moulvibazar, Sylhet, Bangladesh.

His grandson, Maulana Abdullah Al-Nizam Mashoud Majed Choudhury, son of Abdullah Al-Mashoud Fuad Choudhury, is currently continuing the family's spiritual and educational legacy.

Family Genealogy:

Hazrat Shah Champa Baghdadi (R:)
↓
Hazrat Alam Shah
↓
Razzaq Shah
↓
Majlish Jahan
↓
Majlish Mubarak
↓
Majlish Fateh
↓
Sehat Malek
↓
Raju Khan
↓
Yakub Khan
↓
Doost Muhammad Choudhury (of Bhadeshwar)
↓
Muhammad Shafi Choudhury
↓
Muhammad Mukim Choudhury
↓
Muhammad Musim Choudhury
↓
Muhammad Azim Choudhury
↓
Muhammad Abdullah Choudhury (Bhadeshwari Bishkuti)
↓
Muhammad Mashoud Choudhury (Bishkuti)
↓
Nizamuddin Choudhury (Bishkuti)
↓
Abdullah Al Mashoud Fuad Choudhury
↓
Abdullah Al Nizam Mashoud Majed Choudhury

Shah Sufi Syed Muhammad Madani Al-Hussaini – Chief Judge of Medina

The movement led by Abdul Wahhab was advancing rapidly in Arabia, abandoning the path shown by the Prophet. When the soldiers of the movement chose the path of violence, hatred and extremism instead of peace and harmony, the chief authority against them was the Qazi (Judge) himself in Medina. At that time, the chief judge of Medina was Shah Sufi Syed Muhammad Madani Al-Hussaini, son of Syed Abbas Al-Hussaini, he was the Mutawalli[21] of Masjid-e-Nabawi.

When the terrorists, who believed in radicalism, were found guilty in the trial of the judge, Qazi Syed Muhammad Madani ordered the death penalty against them. That historic verdict forced Syed Muhammad Madani Al-Hussaini to leave the Arab world. When the Wahhabis tried to kill him, he received the Prophet's instructions in a dream to immediately leave the country and go elsewhere. In a dream, inspired by the Prophet's revelation and the illusion of life, he immediately left his homeland, parents, siblings, environment, and relatives and came to Mecca for an unknown purpose in order to protect himself. There, he first circumambulated the holy Kaaba and finally arrived in Jeddah. Hazrat Shah Sufi boarded a ship to reach his aimless goal. Although the ship started moving towards its destination, he was a aimless passenger. As the events unfolded, the ship sank in the middle of the sea due to mechanical problems and natural disasters. Almost all passengers experience a peaceful death. Syed Muhammad Madani was swaying to the rhythm of the waves from the water. In

[21] A mutawalli is the manager or trustee of a waqf, which is an Islamic charitable endowment. The mutawalli is responsible for overseeing the waqf property and administering it in accordance with Islamic law and the specific terms outlined in the waqf deed.

this difficult time, a large sea fish came to his side, and Syed Muhammad rode on its back.
Surviving certain death by the power of an invisible, infinite power, the fish finally arrived at the Karachi port of the subcontinent, where Syed Madani landed. According to his family members, this incident occurred in 1885. There was a fear of losing his life, although he touched the ground in Karachi, Undivided India. He did not stay there for long. He moved from Karachi to Dhaka. Leaving a place called Nawab Bari in Dhaka, he moved to the historically famous city of Sufi Shah Jalal's Srihatta. He started living in Charia. From Charia, he finally moved to Kanishail in Karimganj district. He left this place too.

The Zamindars of Ujandihi i.e., the descendents of Nawab Jan Muhammad Khan welcomed Shah Sufi Syed Muhammad Madani Al-Hussaini and donated a large amount of land and residential house, where He settled permanently, which is now known as Ujandihi Puran Saheb Bari.

He died in 1900 in his old house in Ujandihi, Karimganj district. On the hillock adjacent to the masjid of that house, there is the holy shrine of Syed Muhammad Madani Saheb. Every year, the holy Isale-Sawab[22] is held here in his memory.

His son's name was Syed Abdul Haque Madani Al-Hussaini (1895-1967) and his grandsons were Maulana Syed Monirul Islam Madani, Syed Muyeenul Islam Madani, Syed Rafiqul Islam Madani & Syed Shafiqul Islam Madani.

Maulana Syed Monirul Islam Madani Al-Hussaini has only one son, Maulana Syed Mustaque Ahmed

[22] Death Anniversary

Madani, who serves as the President of Latifia Dar-ul-Qirat Samiti, Bharat.

Syed Rafiqul Islam Madani's Al-Hussaini's elder son is Maulana Syed Juned Ahmed Madani, who has served several times as the President of Northeast Ahle Sunnat-wal-Jamat.

Hazrat Konu Shah (1814–1911) – The Mystic of Son Beel

Hazrat Konu Shah, a 19th-century Sufi saint, resided at the heart of a hill beside the serene Son Beel. Renowned for his spiritual wisdom and legendary stories of miracles, he devoted his life not only to faith but also to healing through Yunani medicine. People from distant villages came to seek his guidance and remedies. His shrine, nestled in nature, continues to attract devotees who find solace in his memory.

Abu Yusuf Mohammad Yakub Badarpuri (1854–1958)

Abu Yusuf Mohammad Yakub Badarpuri was a renowned Sufi scholar, social reformer, and freedom fighter, born in 1854 in the village of Bundashil, Badarpur, in present-day Karimganj district of Assam. He was the son of Shah Mohammad Basir, a spiritually inclined figure of the region.

He lived a long life of 104 years, passing away in January 1958. His contributions remain etched in the memory of the region and are celebrated as part of Barak Valley's rich religious and cultural heritage.

Education and Early Life:
Yakub Badarpuri pursued Islamic and philosophical education from various eminent centres across India, including:

- Cuttack (then capital of Orissa),
- Calcutta (a major intellectual hub),
- Rampur, known for its Islamic scholarship.

His exposure to these diverse centers of learning profoundly shaped his worldview, combining traditional Islamic values with a strong sense of community upliftment and education.

Institution Builder and Educator:
Returning to Badarpur, he committed himself to social and religious reform through education. He founded several important institutions, particularly in Deorail, a locality near Badarpur:

- Deorail Maktab LP School
- Deorail ME School
- Deorail Senior Madrassa
- Deorail Darul Hadis Title Madrassa
- Two Mosques and One Idgah

These institutions were vital in spreading both modern and religious education in the Barak Valley region, especially among the marginalized sections of society.

Role in Freedom Struggle:

- Abu Yusuf Yakub Badarpuri was an active participant in the Khilafat Movement, aligning with other national movements for India's freedom.
- He used both his spiritual influence and grassroots activism to support the anti-colonial cause.
- His involvement has earned him a place among the unsung heroes of the Indian Freedom Struggle from Assam.

Spiritual Legacy:

- A respected Sufi, Yakub Badarpuri had followers across India and internationally.
- His teachings emphasized compassion, knowledge, and unity, and his khanqah became a place of solace and learning.
- Even today, his spiritual legacy continues through disciples and admirers spread around the globe.

Shams-ul-Ulama Maulana Mojahiduddin Chowdhury (1863 - 18 June 1941) – The Ocean of Knowledge from Malua

Born into the noble landlord family of Chapghat Pargona in Malua, Karimganj, Maulana Mojahiduddin Chowdhury, son of Zamindar Masud Ali Chowdhury, he emerged as one of the most enlightened minds of his time. After early education at Sylhet Government High School, he advanced through Fulbari Madrassa, Calcutta's Aliya University, and Rampur. His brilliance in Islamic jurisprudence earned him teaching positions-first at Madinat-ul-Uloom Nojibia Aliya Madrassa of Kaliganj, then as a lecturer at Calcutta Aliya Madrassa, under British Govt. (now Aliya University). He later became the principal of Sylhet Aliya Madrassa. His younger son is Prof. Golam Yahiya Chowdhury (1910-1979), who served at M.C. College, Sylhet.

In 1894, the British Government conferred upon him the title Shams-ul-Ulama-'The Sun of the Scholars'-a testament to his deep erudition and luminous intellect. He authored several works in Islamic law and passed away at his ancestral home on 18 June 1941. His shrine rests inpeace before the Malua Jam-e-Masjid, where the scent of reverence still lingers in the breeze.

Fakir Arkum Shah (1877-1941)

Fakir Arkum Shah, born in 1877 in Dharadharpur, Sylhet, was a legendary mystic, poet, and spiritual philosopher, deeply rooted in Sufi traditions. Known for his profound spiritual insight and poetic brilliance, he is regarded as one of the most enigmatic Sufi figures of the Barak-Sylhet region.

Arkum Shah was born into an ordinary family and received a basic general education during his early years. He later married Meherjan, but tragically, they had no surviving children. Though they had three sons, Arkum Shah had foreseen their deaths and had foretold that none would survive-a prophecy that, heartbreakingly, came true. Initially, Arkum Shah led a simple life and served as an Imam, offering prayers and engaging in community religious affairs. His spiritual transformation began when he met Maulana Shah Abdul Latif Qadri of Jalopara, Sylhet, a younger scholar who had migrated from Khorasan-a historically significant region spanning present-day northeastern Iran, Afghanistan, Turkmenistan, and beyond. Under Latif Qadri's guidance, Arkum Shah began his serious pursuit of spiritual and religious knowledge.

After the passing of Maulana Latif Qadri, Arkum Shah continued his quest for enlightenment. He traveled to Karimganj to study under the eminent Islamic scholar of the Indian subcontinent of Naqshbandia-Mujaddidiyah order, Allama Abdullah Bhadeshwari Bishkuti, a revered spiritual authority of Bishkut Dargah Sharif. Upon Allama Abdullah's death in 1918, Arkum Shah received spiritual training and Khilafat (succession in Sufi order) from his son and successor, Peer Shah Allama Moshoud Bishkuti, a learned figure with an academic background. Following Shah Moshoud Bishkuti's instructions, Arkum Shah visited his house and further immersed himself in the mystical path-eventually emerging as one of the most celebrated Sufi sages of the region. Arkum Shah was known for his humility, renunciation, and mysterious aura. Despite having spiritual stature and gaining admiration from influential personalities-including Zamindar Jitu Miya of Sylhet Sadar, Well known teacher Taimur Ali, and Aftab Miya Zamindar, who became his disciple-he lived with minimal material possessions. When offered land near their estates, he humbly refused, saying: "Do not give me a place within your home; give me land in a no man's zone."

His close attendant and khadim (caretaker-disciple) was Haji Joynal Ahmed Khan Saheb, who remained withhim through his final years. Fakir Arkum Shah was not only a mystic but also a profound philosopher. His thoughts revolved around divine love, the mystery of existence, and the eternal truths of the soul. He wrote more than 128 mystical songs, including ballads (bhott kobita), that combined Sufi metaphysics with local folk sensibility. His spiritual poetry continues to influence Sufi musical traditions in Bengal and Barak Valley.

Fakir Arkum Shah passed away in 1941, leaving behind a legacy of spiritual wisdom, poetry, and mysticism. His life, deeply intertwined with the traditions of Sufi love and divine seeking, remains immortalized through his songs and the living traditions of his disciples.

Renowned Newspaper Reflecting the Voice of Barak:

1. **Jonoshokti (Weekly)**: Editor – Nibaran Gupta, Silchar
2. **Jaago (Fortnightly)**: Editor – Jawahar Bhattacharjee, Silchar
3. **Dibakar (Weekly)**: Editor – Abul Kalam Mazumdar, Lala, Hailakandi
4. **Dholeshwari (Weekly)**: Editor – Noni Gopal Dey, Hailakandi
5. **Nobojug (Weekly)**: Editor – Rahul Das, Karimganj
6. **Nababarta Prasanga (Daily)**: Editor – Habibur Rahman Choudhury, Karimganj
7. **Noya Cachar (Weekly)**: Editor – Sailesh Kar Purkayastha, Silchar
8. **Pollibani (Fortnightly)**: Editor – Joynul Hoque Mazumdar, Sonai, Cachar
9. **Pathshala (Monthly)**: Editor – Atin Das, Silchar
10. **Prantojyoti (Daily)**: Editor – Jotindra Chandra Dutta, Silchar
11. **Purbosri (Weekly)**: Editor – Dipendra Kumar Das, Silchar
12. **Purbayon (Weekly)**: Editor – Shakti Dhar Choudhury, Hailakandi
13. **Barak (Weekly)**: Editor – A.F. Golam Osmani, Silchar

14. **Barak Probaho (Weekly)**: Editor – Deshbandhu Singh, Silchar
15. **Bartalipi (Weekly)**: Editor – Sonot Koyeri, Silchar
16. **Bharatvivek (Weekly)**: Editor – Moloy Kanti Das, Silchar
17. **Matribhoomi (Weekly)**: Editor – Poritosh Pal Choudhury, Silchar
18. **Muktiprodip (Weekly)**: Editor – Jotindra Mohan Barbhuiya, Silchar
19. **Donka (Weekly)**: Editor – Kipesh Bhattacharjee, Karimganj
20. **Dalim (Weekly)**: Editor – Jwaidur Rahman Mazumdar, Hailakandi
21. **Songhoti (Weekly)**: Editor – Ramesh Kumar Sharma Mazumdar, Silchar
22. **Swadeshbani (Weekly)**: Editor – Monilal Deb, Silchar
23. **Samayik Prasanga (Daily)**: Editor – Toimur Raja Choudhury, Silchar
24. **Surma (Weekly)**: Editor – Badal Shome, Silchar
25. **Sonar Cachar (Daily)**: Editor – Ronobir Roy, Silchar
26. **Shopot (Daily)**: Editor – Kamalendu Bhattacharjee, Silchar
27. **Srihattabani (Weekly)**: Editor – Ramendra Bhattacharjee, Silchar
28. **Jugoshokti (Weekly)**: Editor – Bidubhushan Choudhury, Karimganj
29. **Dainik Jugosonko (Daily)**: Editor – Bijoy Krishna Nath, Silchar
30. **Jugobani (Fortnightly)**: Editor – Dahar Ahmed Mazumdar, Silchar
31. **Hoshiyar (Weekly)**: Editor – Muslim Uddin Barlaskar, Silchar
32. **Anandajyoti (Weekly)**: Editor – Jotindra Lal Goswami, Karimganj
33. **Azaad (Weekly)**: Editor – Kurmoth Ali Barlaskar, Buribail, Cachar
34. **Assam Sports (Krirasamayiki)**: Editor – Chuni Roy, Karimganj

35. **Eitoh Swadesh (Weekly)**: Editor – Taj Uddin Barbhuiya, Sunabari Ghat, Cachar
36. **Karimganj Songhvad (Weekly)**: Editor – J.B. Roy, Karimganj
37. **Cachar Times (Weekly)**: Editor – Bhudeb Bhattacharjee, Silchar
38. **Cachar (Weekly)**: Editor – Sontush Kumar Roy, Hailakandi
39. **Gothi (Daily)**: Editor – Jotin Deb Roy, Silchar

XXIV
Reader's Guide

For Reflection, Dialogue, and Deeper Understanding

Discussion Questions

1. Which chapter resonated with you the most and why? Was it the Language Movement, the story of Sylheti resilience, or the coexistence of faiths?

2. Did any part of the book challenge your existing assumptions about Assam or Barak Valley?
If yes, how did your perspective shift?

3. How does the struggle of Barak Valley mirror other forgotten or marginalized regions in India or beyond?

4. What role does language play in shaping a community's identity, as seen through the Sylheti narrative?

5. Did you find similarities between your hometown and the stories of Barak Valley?
Think about migration, cultural pride, or lack of representation.

6. Can regional languages like Sylheti gain mainstream recognition without losing authenticity?

7. How do borders — geographical and cultural — affect belonging in the Barak Valley?

8. Which historical figure or legacy family mentioned in the book did you find most memorable? Why?

9. Do you see echoes of the Barak Valley's migration stories in your own family history?

10. How do natural elements — rivers, hills, tea gardens — shape both daily life and identity in the valley?

11. Was there a particular quote, poem, or song that stayed with you? Why did it strike you?
12. Do you think Barak Valley's unique voice is well understood outside the Northeast? Why or why not?

13. How can books like this contribute to restoring cultural memory and historical dignity to neglected places?

14. What feelings did the chapter on tourism and landmarks evoke? Did it deepen your curiosity about the region?

15. In what ways does this book balance emotion with historical fact?

16. If you were to write a local history of your own region, what stories would you begin with?

17. Did the stories of 1971 refugees in Karimganj change how you view migration and humanitarian efforts?

18. What role do educational institutions like Jam-e-Uloom Nizamia or Karimganj Govt High School play in shaping regional pride?

19. How has the digital generation in Barak Valley reclaimed identity through media, music, or startups?

20. In what ways can Barak Valley serve as a model of interfaith coexistence in other parts of India?

Reflection Prompts
"We bled for the right to speak. Now, we write for the right to be heard."
— How do you interpret this line in the context of your own cultural or linguistic identity?

Think about a moment when your community was misrepresented or ignored.

— What would your chapter in “Voice of [Your Valley]” look like?

What song, phrase, or story from your culture feels like a ‘living memory’?
— How can it be preserved for the next generation?
If you had to explain Barak Valley to someone who’s never heard of it, which three words would you choose?

Explore Further
—Research the Assam Language Movement of 1961 and its impact on Barak Valley.

—Write your own short essay or poem titled “My Identity, My Soil.”

—Interview a family member or elder about memories of Partition or the 1971 war.

—Create a photo essay capturing life in a Barak town or village.

—Translate a Sylheti proverb and explore its meaning.

—Ask your parents or grandparents about old Sylheti proverbs, lullabies, songs, and wedding traditions - and write them down.

—Begin a personal research project into your family's origin, migration, or contribution to local history - and preserve it as a written memoir, blog, or digital archive.

—Start a conversation with elders in your community about lost words or idioms and create a family or community glossary.

—Create a scrapbook of documents, photos, or oral stories that reflect your family's place in the valley's legacy.

XXV
A Letter to Future Generations

Hey, future children of Barak Valley!

If you're flipping through these pages, we're proud of you already.
It means you cared. It means you paused.
It means someone still wants to know where we came from, and maybe — where we're going.

This book? It's not just about nostalgia. It's not aesthetic sadness.
It's soil, sweat, silence, and truth, from a place that has always been misunderstood, underrated, and unbothered by outside validation.

We lived in Barak Valley that bled quietly.
But it loved loudly in songs, in strikes, in syllables, in street corners, and in whispered "ami tumar kotha bhulchi na" that echoed after curfew hours.

Maybe our Barak Valley is more digitised. Maybe you're swiping left on old grief.
But don't scroll past the roots that hold you up.

Don't let them rename your accent.
Don't shrink your grandmother's stories to a meme.
Don't archive your identity into footnotes.

Carry Barak in your music, your memes, your voice notes, your activism, your algorithms. Make art. Ask questions. Correct history. Build the platforms we didn't have.
And when you feel small, remember, this book believed you'd be here. Because memory isn't vintage. It's power.

We're handing it to you now.
Take it forward, your way.

With love,
One voice from your yesterday.

XXVI
Your Space in the Story

This page is left intentionally blank.

Here, you may write a memory, a name, a place, a poem, a question or even a silence. Something that belongs to you, or is somehow rooted in Barak.
Because memory doesn't end when the book ends. It continues in those who carry it forward.

Take this space. Let Barak remember you too.

Your Name:
City: Date:

Works Cited

1. Saha, Anupama, and Susmita Gupta. "Nepomorpha and Gerromorpha (Hemiptera) Community in the Agricultural Fields of Barak Valley, Assam, North East India." Asian *Journal of Conservation Biology*, vol. 8, no. 2, 2019, pp. 149-158.

2. Mitchell, Colin P. "Tahmāsp I, Second Ruler of the Safavid Dynasty." *Encyclopædia Iranica*, 26 Oct. 2012, iranicaonline.org/articles/tahmasp-i.

3. Choudhury, Dewan Nurul Anwar Hussain. *Sanad Shilalipi*. 10 Feb. 2001, p. 68. Sanad no. T997/319, dated 1 Sha'ban 1074 Hijri / 1663 AD. Records the appointment of Jan Mohammad Khan as Fauzdar of Bihar.

4. "Jan Muhammad Khan." *Wikipedia*, Wikimedia Foundation, Accessed 25 January 2025, https://en.m.wikipedia.org/wiki/Jan_Muhammad_Khan#:~:text=J%C4%81n%20Muhammad%20Kh%C4%81n%20Bah%C4%81dur%20(Bengali,some%20land%20to%20Sylheti%20residents.

5. Syed Mohammad Ali. "*A Chronology of Muslim Faujdars of Sylhet.*" The Proceedings of the All Pakistan History Conference, vol. 1, Karachi: Pakistan Historical Society, p. 280.

6. Sarkar, Jadunath. Studies in Mughal India. Rajesh Publications, 1919. Sarkar, Jadunath. *History of Bengal.*1948. www.cse.iitk.ac.in/users/amit/books/sarkar-1948-history-of-bengal.html.

7. "Shuja-ud-Din Muhammad Khan." *Wikipedia*, Wikimedia Foundation, Accessed 18 February

2025.en.wikipedia.org/wiki/Shuja-ud-Din_Muhammad_Khan.

8. "Shuja-ud-Din Muhammad Khan." *GKToday*, www.gktoday.in/shuja-ud-din-muhammad-khan.

9. Shuja - Ud - Din Muhammad Khan. *Indianetzone*, www.indianetzone.com/shuja__ud__din_muhammad_khan. Accessed 18 February 2025.

10. "Shujauddin Muhammad Khan." *Banglapedia*, 17 June 2021,en.banglapedia.org/index.php/Shujauddin_Muhammad_Khan. Accessed 18 February 2025

11. Briggs, John, translator. *Siyar-ul-Mutakherin*. By Mir Gholam Hussein-Khan Tabtabai, The British East India Company (Madras Army), 1831.

12. “Sarfaraz Khan." *Wikipedia*, Wikimedia Foundation, en.m.wikipedia.org/wiki/Sarfaraz_Khan. Accessed 19 February 2025.

13. The Tomb of Nawab Sarfaraz Khan as It Survives Today."*ResearchGate*, Accessed 19 February 2025. www.researchgate.net/figure/The-tomb-of-Nawab-Sarfaraz-Khan-as-it-survives-today_fig9_371266781.

14. "Sarfaraz Khan: Murshidabad's Forgotten Nawab." Double *Dolphin Blogspot*, 11 July 2018, double-dolphin.blogspot.com/2018/07/sarfaraz-khan-murshidabads-forgotten-nawab.html. Accessed 23 April 2025.

15. "Bengal under the Rule of Nawabs: A Close View." *HistoryDiscussion*,www.historydiscussion.net/history-of-india/history-of-bengal/bengal-under-the-rule-of-nawabs-a-close-view/5931.

16. "History of the Nawabs of Bengal/The Rise of the Nawabs." *Wikibooks*, en.m.wikibooks.org/wiki/History_of_the_Nawabs_of_Bengal/The_Rise_of_the_Nawabs.

17. "Odisha under the Nawabs of Bengal." *History of Odisha*, historyofodisha.in/odisha-under-the-nawabs-of-bengal/#2.

18. "Lutfullah Tabrizi." Wikipedia, Wikimedia Foundation, 31 July 2025, https://en.wikipedia.org/wiki/Lutfullah_Tabrizi. Accessed 21 February 2025.

19. Choudhury, Achyut Charan. *Srihatter Itibritta: Uttarangsho*. Srihatta Sahitya Parishad, 1973. (in Bengali)

20. Choudhury, Abdus Shahid[23] *উজানডিহি দর্পণ* (Ujandihi Darpan). 1958.

21. Government of India. *White Paper on the Crisis in East Pakistan*. Ministry of External Affairs, 1971.

22. United Nations High Commissioner for Refugees (UNHCR). *Refugee Relief in India: 1971-72 Operational Report*. UNHCR, 1972.

23. Raghavan, Srinath. "1971: Refugees, Relief and Indian Foreign Policy." *India Review*, vol. 10, no. 1, 2011, pp. 1-22.

24. Bose, Sarmila. *Dead Reckoning: Memories of the 1971 Bangladesh War*. Hurst & Company, 2011

[23] Migrated from Ujandihi, Karimagnj, Assam to Fulbari, Sylhet.

25. Choudhury, Achyut Charan. *Srihatter Itibritta: Purbangsho* (in Bengali). Originally published 1910. Kolkata: Kotha, 2000, p. 186.

26. "85th Employee of Closed Assam Paper Mills Dies without Treatment." *The Hindu, 24 Apr. 2021,* www.thehindu.com/news/national/85th-employee-of-closed-assam-paper-mills-dies-without-treatment/article34397098.ece.

27. "Staff Suicide Brings to the Fore State of Assam's Dying Paper Mills." *The Indian Express, 2 May 2019,* indianexpress.com/article/india/staff-suicide-assam-dying-paper-mill s-5704206/.

28. "Defunct Cachar Paper Mill Land to House New Tech Centre; Workers Still Await Dues." *The Assam Tribune, 26 Feb. 2025,* assamtribune.com/assam/defunct-cachar-paper-mill-land-to-ho use-new-tech-centre-workers-still-aw ait-dues-1569439.

29. "19 Ex-employees of Mill in Assam Die after Establishment's Closure; Family Members Point to Stress-related Complications." *Firstpost, 17 June 2018,* www.firstpost.com/india/19-ex-employees-of-mill-in-assam-die -after-establishments-closure-family-members-point-to-stress-related-com plications-4528311.html.

30. "Another Closed Paper Mill Staff Dies, Death Toll 131." *The Times of India, 5 Feb. 2025,* timesofindia.indiatimes.com/city/guwahati/another-closed-paper-mill-staff-dies-death-toll-131/articleshow/107453244.cms.

31. Duttchowdhury, Habib Ahmed. *ভারতবর্ষের ইতিহাসে শ্রীহট্টের প্রতাপগড় রাজ্য (The Pratapgarh Kingdom of Shrihatta in the History of India).* Edited and

published by Mustafa Salim, Utso Prokashan, 127 Aziz Super Market (2nd Floor), Shahbagh, Dhaka 1000. ISBN 978-984-97871-7-4.

32. "We Want Rural Assam to Be a Source of Pride, Not Pity: Gaurav Chakraborty."*EastMojo,* www.eastmojo.com/assam/2022/03/15/we-want-rural-assam-to-be-a-source-of-pr ide-not-pity-gaurav-chakraborty/. Accessed 22 April 2025.

33. "Crafting Livelihoods: How Assam's Youth Are Reviving Bamboo and Handloom Traditions." *EastMojo,* www.eastmojo.com/features/2021/11/07/crafting-livelihoods-how-assams-youth-are-reviving-bamboo-and-handloom-traditio ns/. Accessed 9 July 2025.

34. "Moinul Hoque Choudhury." *Wikipedia*, Wikimedia Foundatio. Accessed 24 April 2025. en.wikipedia.org/wiki/Moinul_Hoque_Choudhury.

35. বৈশ্য, পৰেশ (Paresh Baishya). *অসমৰ সংসদীয় ৰাজনীতিৰ ইতিহাস (Asamar Sangsadiya Rajnitir Itihash)*. 1st ed., Rekha Prakashan, 2014. ISBN: 978-93-83611-52-2. Printed by Abhilekha Graphic, Guwahati.

36. লস্কর, আলি হায়দর (Ali Haidar Laskar). *বরাক উপত্যকা ও ইসলাম (Barak Upatyka O Islam*). Hazrat Shahjalal Publication, Nov. 2016. Printed at F.M. Printers, Panjabari Road, Guwahati-37.

37. Press Trust of India. "Govt Withdraws Assamese as Official Language from Barak Valley." *Business Standard India*, 9 Sept. 2014.

38. "List of Parliamentary & Assembly Constituencies (PDF)." *Election Commission of India*, archived from the original (PDF) on 4 May 2006.

39. "Community-Based Ecotourism Initiative Barak River Safari Opens for Tourists." *Pratidin Time, 5 Nov. 2023*, https://www.pratidintime.com/latest-assam-news-breaking-news-assam/community-based-ecotourism-initiative-barak-river-safari-opens-for-tourists. Accessed 9 July 2025.

40. "Cachar District." *Wikipedia*, Wikimedia Foundation, 8 July 2025, https://en.wikipedia.org/wiki/Cachar_district. Accessed 12 June 2025.

41. "A. F. Golam Osmani." *Wikipedia*, Wikimedia Foundation, 30 June 2024, Accessed 15 June 2025. https://en.wikipedia.org/wiki/A._F._Golam_Osmani.

42. "A.F. Golam Osmani (1933–2009)." *Radiance Viewsweekly, 12 Apr. 2009*, https://radianceweekly.net/af-golam-osmani-1933-2009. Accessed 9 July 2025.

43. "Biographical Data – A. F. Golam Osmani." *IndiaPress.org, 1999*, https://www.indiapress.org/election/archives/lok12/biodata/12as06.php. Accessed 17July 2025.

44. "Bengali Language Movement (Barak Valley)." *Wikipedia,* Wikimedia Foundation, 8 July 2025, Accessed 16 June 2025. https://en.wikipedia.org/wiki/Bengali_Language_Movement_(Barak_Valley).

45. Mazumder, Habibullah. *Prominent Muslims of Assam: Brief Biographical Studies.* First published

Nov. 2016. 1st ed., Natun Diganta Prakashani, Jan. 2023. ISBN 978-93-82965-35-0.

46. Duttachowdhury, Habib Ahmed. *ভারতবর্ষের ইতিহাসে বঙ্গদেশের বীরভূম রাজ্যের উত্তরসূরি শ্রীহট্টের বীরশ্রী-মাইজডিহির রাজবংশের ইতিকথা (The History of the Biroshri-Maijdihi Dynasty of Shrihatta, the Successor to the Birbhum Kingdom of Bengal in the History of India).*

47. Barbhuiya, Abdul Sukkur. বরাকের পীর ফকির (Baraker Pir Phakir - A). First published on 14 October 2008, Edited by মোহাম্মদ আব্দুল কাইয়ুম মানিক বড়ভূঁইয়া, Illustrated by অসীমকুমার নাথ বুলি, Arshi Prokashoni, Printed at সুনীতি কম্পিউটার সেন্টার, Tarapur, Silchar-3.

48. Choudhury, Kamruzzaman. *Silsilaye Bishkutee (সিলসিলায়ে বিশকুটি): The Introduction of the Silsila of Allama Muhammad Nizam Uddin Bishkutee (R.A.).* Published by Mamazzad Ahmed Choudhury, 6 Mar. 2016.

49. Talukdar, Dilwar Hussain. "A Study of Sufi Saints in Karimganj District of Assam (1346-1947)." *Pratidhwani the Echo: A Peer-Reviewed International Journal of Humanities & Social Science*, vol. 3, no. 4, Apr. 2015, pp. 73-78. Published by Dept. of Chemistry of Bengali, Karimganj College, Karimganj, Assam. ISSN:2278-5264(Online), 2321-9319 (Print).http://www.thecho.in

50. Hasnat, Abul. *Bishkuti Wali-Awliader Jibon 0 Karamat (বিশকুটি অলি-আউলিয়াদের জীবন ও কারামত)*. Published by Nizamiya Bishkuti Welfare Trust, Aug. 2009.

51. “Abdul Latif Chowdhury Fultali.” *Wikipedia*, Wikimedia Foundation, 28 June 2024, Accessed 22 June 2025.https://en.wikipedia.org/wiki/Abdul_Latif_Chowdhury_Fultali.

52. Choudhury, Kamruzzaman. *Mashayekhe Naqshbandhi (মাশায়েখে নকশবন্দি): The Introduction of Silsila-e Naqshbandiya Mujaddidiya of Saheb Qiblah Allama Fultali (R.A.).* Published by Sayed Muhibul Islam, Ujandi, 7 Feb. 2015.

53. “Hafiz Ahmad Jaunpuri.” *Wikipedia*, Wikimedia Foundation, 30 June 2024, Accessed 22 June 2025. https://en.wikipedia.org/wiki/Hafiz_Ahmad_Jaunpuri.

54. Riaz, Ali. *Faithful Education: Madrassahs in South Asia.* Rutgers University Press, 2008.

55. Das, Aarti (আরতি দাশ). "*বরাক উপত্যকা থেকে প্রকাশিত পত্র-পত্রিকা ও সাহিত্য সাময়িকী*" ["Newspapers and Literary Magazines Published from the Barak Valley"].

Contact the Author

Thank you for reading Voice of Barak Valley.
Your interest in this book means more than words can express.

If you'd like to connect, collaborate, or share your thoughts about the book, feel free to reach out through any of the following platforms:

Email: faaiz.choudhuryy@gmail.com
Website: https://faaizxchoudhury.github.io/faaizchoudhury/
Instagram: @faaiz.__
Facebook: Faaiz Choudhury
LinkedIn: Muazzaz Ahmed Choudhury (Faaiz)

I welcome readers, students, journalists, and fellow storytellers to start a conversation.

Your voice, like ours, matters.

Get Involved & Share Feedback
Share your thoughts on social media using hashtags like
#VoiceOfBarakValley | #SylhetiPride | #ProudSylheti

Tag the Author & Share Your Feedback
Whether it's a post, story, reel, or blog, your voice adds to the valley.

We'd love your feedback!
Scan this QR code to share your thoughts on Voice of Barak Valley.

Thank you for your support, your feedback helps regional stories shine!

Barak Valley — A Symphony of Unity

Barak Valley is not just a place on the map —
It is a soul-stirring symphony of cultures, communities, languages, and faiths.
Here, Hindus, Muslims, Christians, Buddhists, Jains — all breathe the same air of harmony,
Laugh in each other's joy, grieve in each other's sorrow,
And together, they light the lamps of every festival.

In an era when divisive narratives seek to fragment society,
Barak rises like a beacon — reminding the nation that:
"Our diversity is not a challenge — it is our greatest strength."

From the fertile fields of agriculture
To the bright minds in our schools,
From thriving local enterprises
To the soul of our literature and art —
Barak moves forward through collective strength and shared dreams.

And at the heart of this vision stands our youth —
The torchbearers of tolerance,
The guardians of unity.

Let us envision a Barak that is inclusive, just, and flourishing —

Where language is honored,
Differences are embraced,
And every soul finds equal opportunity and mutual respect.

As we once stood united for our linguistic identity,
Let us now unite for our shared humanity,
And build a Barak that the world looks up to —
Strong in values, rich in culture, and unwavering in harmony.

Dear Reader,

If you've reached this page, you've journeyed with me through every word, thought, and silence. Thank you for lending your time, heart, and attention.

Every ending holds the seed of a new beginning. If this book has stirred a thought, a memory, or a question in you — let it live on.

The story never truly ends. In every line I wrote, I sought sincerity. In every name and truth I traced, I sought justice.

If a single page helped preserve memory or illuminate spirit, my task is fulfilled.

Let remembrance rise,
let reflection dwell,
and let the story echo—
not just in these pages,
but in the world beyond them.

With gratitude,
Muazzaz Ahmed Choudhury,
Author, Voice of Barak Valley.

9 789334 344998

Printed at Repro India Ltd.